"KEEP SMILING"

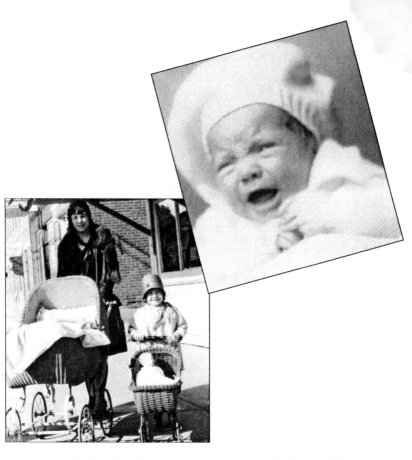

"KEEP SMILING"

A Child's Garden of Reverses

By

ALICE ANN KNISELY

LEATHERS
PUBLISHING

A division of Squire Publishers, Inc.
4500 College Blvd.
Leawood, KS 66211
1/888/888-7696

The author's appreciation and sincere thanks must go to the members of Northwest Arkansas Writers' Guild for their valued encouragement and expertise, 120 Tuesday nights-worth.

ISBN: 1-58597-169-3

Library of Congress Control Number: 2002116389

A division of Squire Publishers, Inc.
4500 College Blvd.
Leawood, KS 66211
1/888/888-7696

REMEMBERING THE MEMORIES

"Alice Ann-don't you-try-to-move-that-chair-it's-too-heavy." Right then she decided that HEAVY was a grown-up word that meant BIG, because the chair was so big. Ever after that, she called it the "heavy chair" and the "heavy table" it pushed up to; also the "heavy room" where it stayed, and the "heavy light" way up in the ceiling. They laughed when she named the "heavy room." Daddy and Mother did. And their best friends: Helen and Doc. And then Thelma and Harvey. But they all started calling it the "heavy room" ever after that. They laughed whenever they said it, and soon enough she knew that heavy didn't always mean big. By that time though, it was too late to change. From then on it was always the "heavy room" where Daddy took pictures of almost everybody in town.

The "heavy room" was the biggest of the rooms in the whole studio. Bigger than the rooms lined up behind it where the cooking and eating and sleeping went on. The "heavy room" had to stay cleaned up all the time. Who knew when customers would come to have their pictures taken? There would be a big boy's First Communion, with a candle in the holder and beads spilling out of a white Bible. The boy would stand in front of the painted background. Daddy would say to stand per-feck-ly still and to tip his chin a little to the left. The boy would fidget, and when he finally stood still, Daddy would say, "Hold it," and sometimes there was a flower in the vase, too.

Alice Ann would be a photographer when she was big. She would hide under the black cloth and say, "Hold it," and then she'd squeeze the little black bulb in her hand and pull out the film frame and tell the mother to come back in a week to see the proofs. That's what she would do.

The floor in the "heavy room" was all covered with battleship green congoleum. She wondered what that meant. Sitting there, cross-legged on it, she had stroked it with her hand and made the words of it go tumbling through her head. Green, she knew. Her favorite color. But congoleum rattled against battleship and didn't make any sense at all.

The string mop was an extension of Mother's arm, dancing wetly around Alice Ann, sitting there. "Alice Ann, don't-you-move-from-that-spot-you'd-slip-on-the-wet-floor-sure-as-anything." So sitting there, the dry space around her was an island that grew smaller as the mop spread its fingers closer and closer. It made the floor as far as could be seen into a deep, dark green ocean of wetness.

Peering over the edge of her dryness, Alice Ann looked down into the dark green and could almost see fishes swimming there. Maybe she would have to sit on her island for a long, long time and everyone would go to supper without her. It would be her favorites:

noodles and chicken and green beans. Ned would eat her tapioca. The wetness would hold her there to the spot until bedtime. They would've done all the family things without her: set the table, say the blessing, pass the gravy, and wash the dishes without her, not even waiting for the floor to dry around her. Then, all of a sudden it was dry. All over the floor of the "heavy room" there was clean, dry green battleship congoleum. And it wasn't even near to suppertime.

Alice Ann knew that being a photographer was magic. The knowing it was something to hug up to herself and feel special about. Ellen Amick's papa was a doctor who made people well again. Junior Moehnert's dad was a lawyer and knew everything about everybody in town, Junior said. The father of Freddie Gdanitz owned the 5 and 10, besides being the town's mayor. But *her* daddy did magic in his studio. He made Forever. On a sign by the studio's big front door, it said: "Photographs are Forever." Mother read it to her and said that Forever was until the end of Time. Daddy made photographs that would last up until the end of Time. That was for sure magic, and it was something to be proud of.

There was a smaller sign hanging right over the lens that you looked into there on Daddy's big portrait camera, when he took your picture. Before she could read, they told her that the sign said, "Keep Smiling." That must be a rule, Alice Ann thought. Why else would it be up where everybody saw it? Maybe it was like the Bible verses on Sunday school bulletin boards and those commands inside the Bible: **Be ye kind** and **Honor your mother and father** and **You shall not kill.** She

3

knew there were more rules she'd learn once they got past Dick and Jane in kindergarten. Then would come the really learning. Until that day, it was enough to watch and listen and tumble it around in your head where the thinking went on.

Most times what grown-ups said could be a real puzzle, so then it was time to turn on the rhyming that could swim inside her head. Word sounds were special, even the ones that didn't make sense. At night they ran all over each other until the sleeping came. Alice Ann tumbled them in and out of her thinking, like **"Piggling-jiggling-diggling"** and **"Robindy-lobindy-bobindy."** Sleeping always came before she could finish the might-be words. Next morning she'd try to remember them all, but they were crowded out by remembering the dreams.

If she thought real hard, Alice Ann could remember being three. That was when Ned was born. All of a sudden he was there in bed with Mother and Doctor Amick was stirring the tapioca on the kitchen stove, where Mother had started it. Ned was a surprise to them all. There wasn't a night-shirt small enough to fit him, he was so teeny. And so red, too. He looked a lot like the baby monkeys at Jenners' Park Zoo. She didn't say it, though. They all said he was beautiful, but no, he wasn't. They carried Ned around on a pillow, so she started carrying Sweet-Baby-Doll on a little pillow, too. By springtime Ned was big enough to hold his head up for a picture, but he screamed bloody murder and pinched his face up, all red and wrinkly. That was all she could remember about him until Ned was tall enough to walk under the kitchen table to

bump his head and find the bread crusts she'd hidden there on little shelves beneath.

One more thing she remembered about being three was when the banks all broke. Grown-ups were really sad when they talked about it, and a man somewhere jumped out of his upstairs window. He was that sad. Alice Ann remembered wanting so much to see the broken bank uptown, but being three meant waiting until somebody could take her across the alley and down to the corner where the bank sat. When she finally saw it, there just wasn't any big crack down the middle, like she'd supposed there should be. She decided that the fixers must've put it back together again, like

Humpty-Dumpty's egg. But she kept still about it.

Being only three had been so hard because of all the things she must wait to grow older to understand. Being laughed at wasn't fun. Sometimes she said things that made everyone laugh. Worse still, then Mother wrote them down in the velvet Baby Book and read them to Helen and Doc. They'd laugh, too. One thing they laughed the most about was when she said, "Ann no like the river. Ann take her bath at home." Someday she would be big enough to understand lots of things and say things that wouldn't make people laugh. She'd be big enough then to laugh at the funny things little kids said. But she decided maybe she wouldn't. Laugh, that is.

※ ※ ※ ※ ※ ※ ※ ※ ※

"Alice Ann, don't-you-breathe-all-over-the-front-door-glass-I-just-got-it-bon-amied-and-wiped-clean." Mother always knew what she was going to do even before she knew it herself. But the door's glass was so nice and cool on her forehead and smelled fresh like the rain. She could stand there and see across the street into the blacksmith shop where Clarence could make sparks fly pounding out a horseshoe or a wagon-wheel rim. Moving her eyes a little, she could then see who it was carrying wicked whiskey out of Ben's LIQUOR EMPORIUM. Next door was ABBY'S CAFE.

Her front door was a lot more special than Jo Ann's or Wilma Jean's. Through hers, Alice Ann could watch exciting things like the Caterpillar road grader doing its job, and gypsies parking their wagons when the carnival came to town. There would always be a tent set up in front of the studio at night, but Daddy wouldn't let them stir off the front step for fear of kidnappers. Like the ones who took the Lindberg baby.

Sundays she had the front step of the studio all to herself. Everything downtown was quiet, especially on their side street. It was so nice to know that not even one customer was coming to do business with Daddy. Oh, unless one of the Aunts for a free sitting. Alice Ann's dolls and doll clothes and doll dishes could be spread out on the woodenness of the step, all smooth from so many people walking on it. That way there weren't slivers to worry about sticking her bottom; the dirt where the boards came together was all packed together and hard as stone.

Mother's old tea towel for a table-cloth had to be smoothed just so before she set out the little tin tea pot and cups and saucers and creamer for the dolls. They sat there: Sweet-Baby-Doll and Nancy-Belle and Lora-Lee, watching the pretend feast of pretend sandwiches and pretend angel food cake. Their glass eyes didn't blink and their painted-on smiles kept smiling like the sign over the camera said to.

When she was all grown up and a lady, Alice Ann would have the American Legion Auxiliary over for tea. They would all smile and set their pocketbooks beside their chairs and talk together and wipe their crumbs off with cloth napkins embroidered in the corners. She would walk to each lady, carrying the rose-on-the-handle teapot very carefully so as not to spill. Each lady would say, "Yes, dear, just a tad more, and "It's sooo delicious." When Mother had the meeting and Alice Ann got to hand out the napkins, Mrs. Mabel Leschinsky would always grab to hug her up tight to her bosom and squeal, "Ooooo, I do wish I had a little red-haired girly like you, Alice Ann!" She smelled like a closet and her chins bobbled over her lace collar, and Alice Ann knew she mustn't squirm. Mother's look was enough to keep her smiling.

* * * * * * * * *

Once, when she was maybe four-going-on-kindergarten, a very strange thing happened. Alice Ann heard Mother's voice, plain as anything, but kind of far away. She remembered what it was like when Mother called her in from play: "Alice Ann!" She turned around and looked, but nobody was there, in the "heavy room" with her paper dolls. Into the bedroom and then the bathroom and the kitchen, but Mother wasn't anywhere inside. Alice Ann finally found her outside at the clothesline, and she said, "Here I am." Mother said that was nice, but no, she hadn't called, and to hand her a clothespin from the basket. How very strange. She knew she'd heard her mother's voice. It had called to her, plain as anything. But Mother didn't play games like that. The voice hadn't come from her, even though it sounded the same. Had it been a dream? No, she was wide awake. The question was: who was it? A customer in the studio? No, there was no one there. A ghost? Maybe. God? Well, maybe it *was* God, sounding like a mother. That almost had to be it.

She knew that God was always watching. Jo Ann's grandma told Jo Ann that God was a great giant eye, always looking down from heaven to see everything that went on down on the earth. Alice Ann tried to think of a very big eye somewhere above her, watching. She tried looking at clouds, hoping to see the eye. But no luck. So, maybe the God Eye was in something she could *already* see. That must be it! Maybe like in the "heavy light" up there in the ceiling of the "heavy room" where customers came to sit for their pictures to be taken.

Lying there on the long, soft bench, underneath the white eye of the "heavy light," Alice Ann tried hard to see God. She lay still, very still for a long time, not even picking the scab on her knee where it itched awfully. She'd kind of liked the taste of her blood when it oozed out. But the God Eye wouldn't like seeing girls eat their scabs. She was almost sure of that. And the skinned-up sore wouldn't get better like it should if she pulled the crusty piece off again. She would stop. She'd stop as long as she was where the big white eye of God could see her doing it.

"Alice Ann, you -come-right-down-from-those-stairs-I-know-you're-there." She never could understand how mothers could tell things like that. It was only the third step leading up to Daddy's frame room and she was all hidden by the solid wooden staircase that followed the stairs all the way up. The other side was bare painted wall without any bannister. The steps weren't so high; they were friendly, wide steps of solid brown-painted wood that always smelled of furniture polish. They were wide enough for Alice Ann to almost lie down on. She would never fall in a million years.

The feeling of being up where she could see things like the grown-ups did was special. It was so hard not to follow the steps up. The window at the foot of the steps was too high to see out of even standing on tiptoe. But sitting on the third step, Alice Ann could see 'way out the window and over to Aunt Belle next door emptying the slop jar on her hollyhocks. Farther over, Uncle Ashley would be trimming his hedges. Up, up on the steps, she could feel tall.

Growing taller was such a slow thing. She ate the things to make her bigger, like spinach and carrots. Maybe she'd always be short. Like Daddy. He was the shortest man around. Daddy was so short that grownups called him "Stub," like an itty bit of a pencil all used up. Grandma C said that Daddy had been real sick as a little boy and didn't grow as big as he should have. Alice Ann tried to think up Daddy as a little boy. Little, like her. Still too short to see out the window. Maybe that was the reason he never did tell Mother when he came down from the frame room and found Alice Ann on the third step, or maybe even number four. He just smiled, like they had a secret together. Then he stepped over her, lifting his framed picture high above her. Most times then, she would come down a step, just in case he thought like Mother did that she'd fall. But she knew she wouldn't. Fall.

Most of all, she wouldn't get sick with whatever had made Daddy short. She thought a long time about that, sitting there with her knees scrunched up against her tummy, her back against step number four. The steps somehow seemed to call to her to come higher and higher. It was just so easy to raise her bottom until she stood up, then to simply sit on number four, pull up her knees again and go one more.

When she was First Grade, Alice Ann decided she would be tall enough to step up all the steps like Daddy did. Then she could see the magic in the frame room where Daddy made big wooden frames and cut the glass for them with a special cutter. When he brought them downstairs, Mother would put wet Bon Ami all over the glass. When it dried, she would wipe the glass with a dry cloth all over and into the very corners where her fingers nibbled out even the ittiest bit of Bon Ami. Alice Ann wanted to help do it. When she was big, she'd even make the frames and cut the glass and clean it off and help Daddy a great big bunch. She would go stepping all the way up to the frame room. And she'd never fall.

There was one day when she came awfully close to falling. It was when her chin was high enough to clear the window sill, but she still went up step number three. By twisting a bit and leaning over, Alice Ann could get her elbows braced on the sill. She could see 'way down the street then. That was when she saw the strange-looking man who wasn't walking straight. He wobbled like he couldn't decide which way to go, and the closer he came the more she leaned into the window screen and almost tumbled down the three steps. But she didn't. Alice Ann hurried down and out to the front desk where Daddy was adding up numbers. She wanted to see the man walking crooked in front of the studio. So did Daddy. He took one look and told her to go 'way back to the kitchen.

Walking backwards and slowly, she could watch Daddy run outside and stop the man. He looked like someone she knew, kind of, but his hat was pulled down over his face. When Daddy got the man to come into the studio, Alice Ann heard them talking. The man was Harvey who did the painting on the studio walls and hung the wallpaper in the kitchen. He wasn't joking though, like he always did. He was crying! Then Daddy brought Harvey back into the kitchen and shooed Alice Ann out into the back yard, but not before she saw him put on the perk-o-later for coffee and sit Harvey down with a clean handkerchief for his tears. She never did get to find out why Harvey cried.

Sitting in the swing and thinking about it, Alice Ann wondered a lot about what could have made Harvey sad enough to cry and walk crooked. She counted her swingings up to seventy-nine and then went back into the kitchen where Mother was now, and no Harvey. Before she could ask a question, Mother said Harvey was sick. Daddy slammed the coffee pot down hard and said, "Sick, nothing! Harvey was *DRUNK!* Drunk as a skunk! But now he's better. Let's get on with it."

While Alice Ann got on with it, she still did a lot of wondering. She had heard before about drunk. There had been a big empty green bottle lying on the sidewalk, and she'd heard the Gzehoviak boy call it a "dead soldier," while he held his nose and wobbled the way Harvey had done. Somehow, those two things were connected to each other, but she wasn't sure just how. Drunk must come out of green bottles, and maybe skunks found little bits of drunk in the green bottles lying around. It was for sure something to remember and understand when she was big. When she was grown-up and saw a drunk person, she would do just what Daddy did; she'd get them a cup of coffee to make them feel better. It had been a good thing for Daddy to do. Maybe Harvey had been sick like Mother said, and drunk, too. Alice Ann wouldn't ask questions about it just now. She would file it away in her thinking and remember it as "the day I saw my first drunk man."

＊ ＊ ＊ ＊ ＊ ＊ ＊ ＊ ＊ ＊

"Alice Ann, don't-you-let-me-see-you-picking-that-sore-on-your-nose-again." She heard Mother say that ten times a day. It was a mother thing, she guessed. Something to be careful about. So Alice Ann was very careful not to let Mother or Daddy see her picking it. Hiding 'way back in the pantry, behind the ironing board, sometimes she would (oh, so carefully) peel the big scab off the end of her nose. When it itched, she figured maybe that was a sign that the scab needed a little help to come off.

The nose scab hadn't started out to be big, but it got that way easy. One day Paul called her "Freckle Face" and grinned his bigger-than-you-cousin grin and pointed at the brownish-red blotch almost sitting on the very end of Alice Ann's nose. Out in the summer sun so much, her face and neck and arms and legs were filled with lots and lots of freckles.

"Oh, Alice Ann, you-were-sure-to-have-your-Grand-mother-Potter's-hair-and-coloring," Mother said a little sadly. Then she told of how "Mammy" had worn a big floppy hat on her head and long white stockings over her arms whenever she went out in the sun. But who would want to be covered up and hot in the noon-day sun? The sun felt good on bare skin. Maybe if she stayed out a long time and got loads of freckles, they would all run together and she'd be tan everywhere like Virginia Vincent was.

Until she was all-over freckles, Alice Ann didn't want that great big one on the end of her nose. One day, all

13

alone in the bathroom, she scraped and scraped until the ugly thing came off, with a bunch of blood that needed wiping and then more wiping. Later came a scab to cover up the place where the freckle had been. It wasn't as red as the freckle, but it itched and puffed up so that she could see it even without a mirror if she crossed her eyes and looked square down at it.

There were other kids with freckles, mostly kids with red hair like hers. And in summer she saw kids with nice dark brown skin that might've been freckles once. Alice Ann hoped that was the way it turned out. Picking off the scab from her nose took up a lot of time. Sometimes she forgot all about it, but then Mother would say her "don't-let-me-see-you-picking" speech and Alice Ann remembered that the pesky thing was still there, big and crusty.

One day her whole nose hurt a lot. It looked bigger, like Jiggs's in the funny paper, and it was sore to touch. That was the day Mother decided about going to see Dr. Wanek about it. She said, "Alice Ann, your-nose-is-infected-for-sure," whatever that meant. She said that maybe it would need to be "lanced," whatever *that* meant. It didn't sound good, and she was sorry that she'd tried to take the freckle off her nose. On the way to the doctor's office, holding on tight to Daddy's hand, Alice Ann got sorrier and sorrier. As they went up the steep stairs to the office above the bank, she wanted to say to turn around and go home and she'd promise never, *never* to pick off the scab again. Daddy's closed-up, worried face made her somehow keep quiet.

It was hard to sit still in Dr. Wanek's waiting room. His couch was slippery enough to keep sliding off. There was a big medicine smell, stronger than the stuff Daddy used to rinse out his mouth. Pretty soon Dr. Wanek was lifting her up onto a table in his office, squeezing her nose until her eyes watered, saying "Hmmm" and then "Hmmm," and whispering to Daddy with a smile. There was a kind of pounding inside her nose, especially when Dr. Wanek wiped it with a wad of cotton on a stick. Then came the wooden stick with black, goopy stuff that stuck to her nose and smelled so icky she thought she'd throw up.

In the mirror on the door Alice Ann looked HORRIBLE. The black goop covering her nose was much worse looking than the big freckle had been! It was very hard not to cry. Daddy still looked stern and frowny, making it hard to come right out and say she was sorry. She knew he was thinking that he didn't want to walk down the street with her and the black nose. People would stare and maybe laugh. Maybe he would go on ahead and she could walk behind or even wait until night-time to go home. She wondered if she'd be able to find the way back to the studio all by herself.

Slowly together they went down the stairs and stopped at the landing. Daddy opened the outside door and stepped into the sunshine. He beckoned to Alice Ann to follow, so she reached out her hand and he took it in his. Down the stone steps and onto the sidewalk, wouldn't you know? There were lots of people coming toward them. She wanted the sidewalk to open up right then and there and drop her down into a deep hole. Alice Ann looked at Daddy and he was smiling and nodding to the ladies and men they met, walking along just like he was out for a Sunday stroll with his little girl. She knew how awful she looked; she wouldn't blame him if he all of a sudden walked away real fast, but still he held tight onto her hand while they made their way back to the studio. It was all a wonderment. Most daddies wouldn't have done what hers had: walk along with his ugly daughter just as if she were a beautiful princess.

She would never in a million years forget this day, it was that special. She'd never try to get rid of freckles either, even if they didn't grow altogether. She would never bother them again. But if she was God, she'd never have invented freckles!

LIVING THE LEARNING

It was easy to tell from its beginning that this was not going to be a "Keep Smiling" day. When her bare feet touched the cold linoleum, she heard Daddy scolding the oil burner. Somehow she had the feeling that this day was one to worry about. Mostly to worry over was The Service. All of yesterday she'd heard the grown-ups whispering about it, and the day before that when the Aunts came over, they all cried into their hankies without stopping.

Alice Ann had a bunch of questions stored up to ask, but Mother kept her mouth tight all the time which meant: "Absolutely-no-questions-today." Daddy left the studio early in the morning and locked the studio front door where he hung a sign that said: CLOSED TODAY for THE SERVICE.

It was hard not to know anything except that today was The Service. She stayed in the bathroom with the 'lectric heater on full blast longer than she should've. Then she had to stand up to eat her Dwarfies from a bowl on Ned's high chair tray because the kitchen table was piled up with pies and cakes people brought. Still wondering about The Service, she sat with Ned until he did Number Two for sure. The wondering didn't stop while she dressed him in the wooly romper suit he only wore to Sunday School. It was for sure a "No Smiling Day" with dark skies and rain turning into snow so they had to wear their floppy overshoes to Aunt Netta's house for The Service. She hoped Paul would be there.

The Service had something to do with Grandma C.'s being sick for a long time. She figured that's why everybody was looking cross and sad at the same time. Thinking about being sick made her feel sad, too. Ned wasn't sad, but his nose kept running and his eyes were blurry enough for him to look sad like everyone around them. Alice Ann wondered if she should be crying and sad, too.

Once, when she went to the closet for her nightie, Alice Ann had found Mother standing far back in the corner and crying kind of quiet-like, but loud enough to hear. It had been a strange sound, her mother crying. Mothers never did cry, even when they burned their arms on hot irons. It was too different to hear the crying and Alice Ann wanted it to stop, so she went closer and put her arms to touch Mother. It seemed like the right thing to do, but right away she was pushed back, kind of rough-like. Somehow it had been a bad mistake to even come to the closet. There was something in her throat, hard and tight, and it took a very long time to try to go sleep that night, wondering what had happened to make Mother cry.

When they got to Aunt Netta's house where The Service would be, she wanted like everything to go play with Paul, but the grown-ups made them sit on chairs in the kitchen and watch them drink coffee and talk whispery again. It was very hard to keep quiet, but she knew enough to do it. Ned's nose needed wiping a dozen times before Mother came to pick him up. About that time, Daddy motioned for Alice Ann to follow him out of the kitchen. Together, hand in hand, they walked into Aunt Netta's parlor room always before kept closed up tight. Today it was open and filled up with lots of flowers, mostly roses. Sure enough, there were roses all over the place, in vases and in big, tall baskets. The strong roses smell came over and around and behind her, so much that her eyes watered and her nose felt wrinkly and she couldn't get a big, deep breath, try as she did. There was way too much roses smell and she said so, turning to go back to the kitchen.

All of a sudden Daddy was picking her up and lifting her high enough to look down into a great, long box filled with silky material. Somebody was lying in the box, all dressed up and like sleeping. Then Daddy was crying. He was crying big crocodile tears, and between the cryings he said to her, "Doesn't Gramma look just like a doll?"

Alice Ann squirmed in Daddy's arms and turned her head into his shoulder. She wanted to yell at him, "NO! She sure doesn't look like a doll at all, at all!" Dolls were little and pretty and smiling. The person in the box was a wrinkled old lady with painted cheeks. She didn't look anything like the Grandma C. that Alice Ann remembered. She wasn't moving either, to open her eyes. Then Alice Ann knew she must be like Lucky was after the car hit him. Dead. Dead as a doornail, like Harvey said when he carried Lucky away to bury him. Grandma C's being dead had made everybody sad. Her being dead had made Daddy cry, something Alice Ann had never seen before. It wasn't a good thing for her to do. It was something Alice Ann would never forget. Not in a million years. Not ever. She could never forgive Grandma C. for that. She would never want to smell roses again. There were too many roses. Too much crying. Too much dead. It was for sure something never, never to forget.

* * * * * * * * *

All summer long, Alice Ann had known that they would start Kindergarten without her. Mother had told her that. When Jo Ann and Honey Lou and Lois were deciding which pencil box to buy at Gdanitz's Five and Ten, she knew that there was no hurry to buy hers. She couldn't use it until she was five in November. Daddy said it was the Law that she wasn't to start school until she was five, and the Laws were never to be broken, no matter how hard it was to obey them.

"Alice Ann, you-start-being-a-Kindergartner-*only*-when-you-have-your-number-five-birthday," Mother said it many times. She didn't need to remind Alice Ann; the reminder was there when she watched Honey Lou walk past the studio that first day of school, carrying her Tom Mix pencil box. And even after that, it stayed in Honey Lou's very own desk in the Kindergarten room, along with her Big Chief tablet.

The days after that were long and longer, even though Mother said they were getting shorter. It was so hard to be what Mother called "patient." There were only Ned and Charles to play with. Alice Ann got awfully tired of being with those babies. That's what they were. Babies. Charles snuffled all the time and never had a handkerchief. His nose drippings ran down his chin and onto his neck in gloppy little rivers, and she got tired of always wiping his face. Charles hated her making him blow his nose into one of Daddy's big handkerchiefs. He just kept snuffling.

There were times when Charles bullied Ned, since he was bigger and a year older. Alice Ann didn't like that and she warned him, but he wouldn't listen, so one day she threw his cap 'way up on top of the porch roof. Then Charles bawled and blabbed to Helen, who had a talk with Mother; Alice Ann had to stay inside while the boys made big leaf piles, jumping in and out of them, yelling like wild Indians. It was so hard to wait for November.

When it got closer to her birthday, they went to Gdanitz's for her pencil box. But, wouldn't you know? All of them had been sold. There wasn't one left, even in the store's back room. Swanson's Drug Store was out of them, too. Mother took her to Lewandowsky's General Merchandise for school shoes and asked there, too, about a pencil box, but no luck. There was not one in town. Alice Ann tried hard to keep from crying, and that night she couldn't hold it back to keep smiling. Mother must have heard her because soon she came and sat down beside her. "Never-you-mind-don't-cry-you-will-have-a-pencil-box-to-take-to-school-I'll-make-you-one."

The home-made pencil box wasn't like Honey Lou's or Jo Ann's. She knew it wouldn't be when Mother started gluing the green material all over the top and sides and insides of Grandpa C.'s empty cigar box. It got trimmed with green rick-rack like Mother put around the collar of Alice Ann's first-day-of-school dress. She crocheted a little green hook to fasten over the green button to keep the lid shut. Mother was proud of what she'd made; she showed the box to Daddy and then to Helen and Doc, and they oohed and ahhed and said how lucky Alice Ann was to have a mother who could do all that. It was so hard to smile and hold the green pencil box when she wanted most of all to throw it against the wall and break it into a million pieces. She knew that wouldn't help anything. And she wouldn't have a pencil box to carry to Kindergarten.

Saturday when Jo Ann came to play, she asked if Alice Ann was ready to go with her on Monday and did she have her pencil box all filled with pencils and crayons she'd need? No, but Mother gave her money to buy pencils and even the jumbo box of crayolas with oodles of different colors. She wanted to try them right away but, of course, then they wouldn't have beautiful sharp ends for Kindergarten's first day.

Next day in Sunday School she got to light the candles on the wooden cake, and they all sang the Happy Birthday song. At home there was real frosted angel food cake in the middle of the kitchen table with fried chicken and smashed potatoes and gravy and Helen's puffy rolls. With dinner over, there were presents wrapped in last Sunday's funny paper. Ned gave her a red ruler. Helen and Doc gave her two big erasers and a dear little green pencil sharpener to twist pencils in for sharp ends. Daddy handed her the last, and biggest package. Maybe a puzzle, or a game. While she unwrapped, she thought of things it could be. But what she saw inside made Alice Ann yell out loud enough to make Ned jump.

The present was the most beautiful Shirley Temple pencil box she'd ever seen, with a shiny clasp and dividers for each of the pencils and crayolas and ruler. Mother was wiping her eyes and Daddy was laughing along with Doc. In between chuckles, Daddy told how they'd bought the pencil box way back in September and kept it hidden all the time.

Looking at Mother, Alice Ann wondered about the first green home-made pencil box. She knew that she would never throw it against the wall to smash it. Right then and there, she decided she would keep it forever for all the special things she collected, like the Indian head penny she found, and funny-shaped rock from Dead-Horse Creek and her Sunday School best attendance pin. Things like that needed a very special place to keep from being lost.

That night after God-blesses, she gave thanks for being five finally and getting to start Kindergarten and having the most beautiful pencil box anybody could ever have. And Alice Ann decided that once she learned to write, she would tell about the wonderful day of the Shirley Temple pencil box.

* * * * * * * * * *

"Alice Ann, you-know-better-than-to-come-out-of-the-bathroom-still-pulling-up-your-panties." Mother said it in her whispery voice that meant a Customer was out in front being waited on, maybe even someone in for a Sitting. So she knew to act "proper." She didn't very often come out with her pants down, only when she was in a big hurry. And Jo Ann said that calling them "panties" was for babies.

This time coming out soon had a good reason. The developer smell from Daddy's darkroom was so awful strong, that Alice Ann had to rush out once she was done with her "business." Even with the bathroom door to the darkroom tight shut, the stronger than any medicine smell came right in under the door. She had to get out quick or else she'd "erp."

Most times the darkroom chemical smell wasn't so strong. Most times there was the fresh cold water smell coming from the rinsing cage that turned round and round, tossing the prints against each other to clean off the chemicals that had helped to make them into pictures. Sometimes there was the warm blanket smell from the little electric heater, and the shiny smell of new print paper just opened, ready to begin making magic at Daddy's printer or enlarger.

If the paper was lying there open to be used, all the lights were turned off, except for the glow from the printer's bulb and the hanging-down red light from above the developing tanks. Darkness in the darkroom had never been scary to Alice Ann. Maybe it was because even when she was real little, Daddy let her come in and walk over to where his voice was. She could touch his pant leg and know that he was standing there at the developing trays, moving paper pieces around in the special stuff that made pictures come.

Sometimes she just closed her eyes and went in the direction of Daddy, swimming through the darkness with arms outstretched until she touched him. He would know she was there, since to get in she had to call from the connecting bathroom to find out if it was all right to walk in. She knew the rules by the time she was big enough to reach the door knob. The bathroom door out to the bedroom had to be shut tight with the bathroom light off for sure.

Once inside the darkroom, sometimes she would sit on a little stool there in the darkness out of the way, listening to the quietness, with all-around darkness, feeling safe and happy and kind of special. Mother wondered about that. Alice Ann couldn't explain how it just seemed the right thing to do. She and Daddy didn't talk very often. They weren't Talkers like Mother and Aunt Belle and Aunt Netta who talked a lot, sometimes all at the same time, not even listening to each other, just talking on and on.

Alice Ann decided that she would be a Listener like Daddy. It was a good way to find out about things, especially what she had trouble understanding. It seemed better to be quiet and listen, to keep the things she heard all piled up in her head to take out when she was bigger and smarter. Then would be the time to figure out what the things meant. It was a good idea not to ask too many questions when she came into a room and grown-ups stopped talking all of a sudden about grown-up things. Things like Thelma and Harvey upstairs over the bank. That's where Thelma had her apartment and her beauty shop. She made ladies look beautiful with Marcels and Revlon nail polish. Mother didn't need to get beautiful, but Helen went every Monday afternoon to Thelma's beauty shop and then always stopped by at the studio, smelling even sweeter than baby powder and looking all curled and shiny.

Thelma came over for supper sometimes, and she

would talk to Alice Ann just like they were both ladies. Once she showed how to make a knot in the end of thread by squeezing the thread into a little ball and pulling real quick. Most times there was a knot just like magic, lots easier than tying it. Thelma started embroidering a dish towel for Alice Ann to finish and give to Mother. It was a secret between the two of them, and Mother would be so surprised on her birthday when she opened the package. Would she believe that Alice Ann had done almost all the hemming around the edge? Thelma smiled and said sure she would.

There was still something to wonder about, though. It was Thelma and Harvey. One hot night they sat out on the front step of the studio after supper. Mother brought out folding chairs for Aunt Belle and Aunt Netta to sit on. None of them wanted to stay inside on such a hot summer night. Before she came out, standing at the door, Alice Ann heard the talk about "what-went-on-up-there" with Mother nodding her head up toward the apartment across the street where Thelma lived and did her beauty shop things. The what-went-on-up-there talk stopped when the Aunts and Mother saw Alice Ann coming out. They put their fingers to their lips and smiled a kind of secret smile. Then Aunt Belle whispered, "Little pitchers have big ears," whatever that meant. And all of a sudden they all started talking about when it would rain.

She looked across the street to past Ben's Liquor Emporium and the Chat 'n' Nibble Cafe. That was where the steps led up to the apartments. Thelma's came first, so her windows were first, looking out on the street. At night when her lamp was on, you could see through her lace curtains and someone moving around, then pulling down the shades. Alice Ann knew that "what-went-on-up-there" was Thelma doing the supper dishes with sometimes Harvey stacking them in the cupboard for her, and then maybe turning on the radio for "Amos and Andy." Or "Fred Allen." Sometimes there was just music, and Thelma and Harvey would dance past the window, before someone pulled down the shades.

It was a good thing for Thelma to have a friend like Harvey, she thought. People needed friends. Even grown-ups needed friends, that was for sure.

Alice Ann first heard the word from Aunt Netta. It was a new, grown-up word she liked rolling around on her tongue and then inside her head. "Worry-some." It was really two words, but the way grown-ups said it made it one word. Aunt Netta's days must have had some worry in them, the way she said it and shook her head kind of sadly. Worry-some must have had something to do with Uncle Jim and his being out of a job lots of the time, and his "hitting the bottle," whatever that meant.

It would be nice, she decided, if *all* grown-up words were plain enough to understand, like worry-some. Alice Ann would like that. It was fun to use grown-up words, but so many of the good-sounding ones were hard to remember when to use.

She was sure that being a hero was kind of worry-some, at least to her. The reason for being called a hero and then feeling worry-some was Ned and the china cupboard at Mammy's house that summer. Little brothers could be pests, she could agree with Ellen, but Ned wasn't so bad, especially when there was no one else to play with. "Alice Ann, you-need-to-be-a-good-example-to-Ned-he-looks-up-to-you" was one of Mother's favorite sayings. She thought she knew what *example* meant, but that was another one of those grown-up words you could wonder about. She liked having a brother better than Ellen did, that was for sure. The accident, though, made her wonder if brothers were worth the trouble.

It turned out to be an accident where nobody got hurt bad. She was real glad of that. Like Mammy said, it could have been a *catastrophe*. Now there was another wonderful grown-up word! When Alice Ann saw Ned swinging on the half-open door of Mammy's china closet, she was kind of sure it was a very bad idea. It wasn't in a closet, but standing on legs by itself there in the living room with long doors that swung out if they weren't latched tight. And there weren't any grown-ups around to tell Ned that a three-year-old was too big to be doing it, and that's when the thing happened, with the door swinging 'way out and Ned hanging on for dear life, and the china closet giving a little thump with its back legs. It was scary.

By the time Alice Ann got to him, Ned had let loose of the door, but he was just standing there like a statue, looking up at the whole big china closet tipping over and dishes starting to fall out in a big rush. Things were seeming to move in a slowed-up way until Alice Ann ran to reach up and stop everything from coming down on top of them.

She wasn't sure how Grandpa knew what was going on, but all of a sudden he was there beside them with the dishes falling all around and Ned bawling his eyes out and the china closet not crashing down like she thought for sure it would. When Alice Ann opened her eyes, the shelves were empty and all over the floor

was brokenness. There was one cup still whole and rolling on the floor away from them.

Grandpa went to the store and bought big white heavy cups and saucers and plates for them to use. She went along with him, and that was when her worrysome time started. He told everybody in the store and even out on the sidewalk how his granddaughter was a real hero. It made her feel all hot and sweaty and embarrassed. Alice Ann didn't feel anything like a hero. Down deep she knew that she should have been watching Ned to see that he didn't swing on the china closet doors and get all of Mammy's good china dishes broken. It was a real worry-some feeling to be called a hero. She wanted them all to forget about it. Mother didn't say that Alice Ann was a hero. If she had, it would be easier to believe. If Grandpa hadn't come when he did, both she and Ned would've been flat as pancakes under the china closet. She was sure of that. Every time they drank their cocoa from the big white heavy cups, Alice Ann was reminded of it.

* * * * * * * * * *

It was sure to be a keep smiling day whenever Paul got to come over to play at the studio. Aunt Netta always said he "came out laughing," whatever that meant. And whenever Alice Ann and Paul came out of his house, they sure enough were laughing. Always. Paul was so funny. He could "bug" his eyes 'way out and roll them around and back into his head where you couldn't see them. She could never hold back the giggles, even when they were there in the studio's biggest room and there might be customers out in front being waited on. She had to stuff her hankie clear into her mouth to be quiet. And that made Paul look even funnier.

"Alice Ann-don't-you-and-Paul-give-Daddy-any-problems-while-we're-gone-to-Legion-Auxiliary." Mother said it, walking out the front door with Aunt Netta. Paul looked at Alice Ann and she looked back at him, wondering what kind of problems they might find. There wasn't much to do inside the studio, except maybe gather up all the empty film spools from the trash barrel in the darkroom. They could be stacked on top of each other to form towers before they all came crashing down without as much noise as she'd hoped. But then the spools rolled every which way and it took forever to find out where they'd all scooted to.

Hiding behind the movable white background and listening for customers to come in, they made strange, funny noises, like Paul burping giant burps any old

30

time he wanted. Alice Ann tried to, but they always came out like hiccups and, of course, they had to giggle and poke each other until Daddy found them and said to go swing in the backyard.

Harvey and Uncle Jim had put up the swing. It had taken a long time to do it, because they argued about how to brace the poles and how strong the chain should be and how deep the holes should be for the poles; all sorts of special arguings, until it seemed like they'd never get it done. And finally the swing stood there, just inside the low fence that was the lot line. You could swing 'way high enough to be up in the air over the lot line for a minute and look down on the fence to count lady bugs crawling there.

Paul said because his dad, Uncle Jim, had helped put up the swing, it partly belonged to him. That didn't seem fair. Paul had a tire swing in his yard, but it wouldn't swing up very high, only whirl round and round 'til they were dizzy enough to walk like drunk men.

Alice Ann's swing would go real high if she pumped very hard. When Paul was over, they took turns, but he always kept his turn going longer since his dad had helped put it up. He was a whole year older and she didn't argue, especially since that certain day he had Lifesavers in his pocket. They saw who could keep the candy piece the longest in your mouth, and Alice Ann almost always won by sucking real slow. The red ones tasted so good, it was hard to keep them on your tongue without quick sucking the goodness out of them.

Next time it was her turn to swing, Alice Ann still had the red Lifesaver in her mouth. The real fun was to swing high enough to open your mouth just a little and let the wind whistle through the Lifesaver's hole.

Then it made a little whispery sound, 'way up in the air, just like a bird.

"Look at me and hear my bird sound," she started to say, but something happened to the candy all of a sudden. It swooped back into her mouth where she couldn't even reach it with her tongue. It stuck. There it sat like a big stone in the place where she wanted to swallow. Being too big to swallow and too stuck to cough out started to get kind of scary. It was hard to slow down the swinging and stop to get out and tell Paul what was happening. He looked at her and just laughed when she pointed to her mouth, trying to talk. It was getting very hard to make some breath come out and tell him what was wrong. Even down on her knees, trying to spit, nothing would happen like it should. Alice Ann felt like crying, but the crying wouldn't even come out.

All of a sudden Paul ran to wherever Daddy was, and when they got there, the sky turned dark even with the sun shining. Daddy's face close to hers was all blurry, and her head seemed fat enough to burst open. Nothing would come out of her mouth, especially the Lifesaver. Pounding on her back didn't help; that's what Daddy did first. Then he turned her upside down, but no luck. Maybe she'd always have the Lifesaver in her mouth. Maybe she'd die without any air. Maybe she'd never get to be seven. Maybe Mother would be real mad about her swinging with candy in her mouth.

All at once she was in the kitchen and Daddy was at the telephone and everything was dark. She felt tight and dreamy and scared all at the same time. Then Daddy was pouring hot water into her mouth, down her chin, into her nose, and down her neck, saying that's what Doctor Amick said to do. Soon the Lifesaver was small enough to come out and the kitchen light was back on and she knew she wouldn't die after all.

Swallowing felt so good. She swallowed and swallowed and swallowed some more. Paul came over close and bugged his eyes out to make her smile. Daddy said it was "a close call" and made Paul throw away the rest of the Lifesavers, even the red ones. Alice Ann guessed maybe they were one of the problems that Mother was afraid of when she went off to Auxiliary. And sure as anything, she'd find out all about it. So would Aunt Netta. So would Uncle Jim. Paul said that he would get "swatted: for sure. But Alice Ann knew it was all her fault. Swinging kids should never eat candy.

* * * * * * * * * *

If Mother said it once, she said it two hundred times. It was just one more of those Mother-things: "Alice Ann-I-just-want-you-to-think-about-it. I-want-you-to-think-long-and-hard-about-it." Once you began thinking about just anything long and hard, it *was* hard.

Most times, Alice Ann knew what Mother wanted her to think about. She remembered having to think long and hard about being spanked in Kindergarten. She'd known that it wasn't something that should ever happen. But it did. It for sure happened. She rolled it back in her head many times, and it wasn't fun to think about it, long and hard, or even short and quick.

She wasn't the only one to get spanked. Lois Bartunek got spanked, too. It was Lois' ruby ring they took off to look at and didn't mean to drop it. But it rolled all the way under Miss Andersen's deck when they knew they should be paying attention to the reading in the Elson Reader. All of a sudden it was Alice Ann's turn, and in that same all of a sudden she knew that she hadn't listened to whoever read before her turn. There was a very big quiet time. Miss Andersen got all red in her face about it. Maybe she got so red because Kindergarten was having Company that day. Harold's mother and Jo Ann's mother came to school to visit Kindergarten especially, to see what happened there. What happened that day was Lois Bartunek and Alice Ann Conger got spanked.

The worst punishment, worse than Miss Andersen turning her over her knee and whopping, was going home afterward and telling Mother.

"Alice Ann, that should-never-have-happened-you-know." It sure shouldn't have, but it did. The spanking was punishment, a big word that grown-ups were fond of saying. Ordinarily, it would have been an interesting word to hang onto and use sometime, but it seemed like a big heavy necklace hanging around her neck.

Walking part-way home together, Lois told that she was sure to get another spanking when she got home. There in the kitchen, after telling, it was very quiet for a long time while Mother pulled down the diapers from the line that hung there on rainy days. She folded them ever so carefully and put them in the basket before she said the "think-about-it-long-and-hard" thing. She said it in a different voice, one kind of between laughing and crying.

There wasn't a spanking at home then, not like Lois Bartunek said there would be; but there *was* going to bed right after supper, with no bath or tooth-brushing. Mother and Daddy talked in soft voices back in the kitchen, too soft to be heard, and later Alice Ann thought she heard the sound of Daddy laughing. But that couldn't be; a spanking in Kindergarten was nothing to laugh about. In her "Now I Lay Me" she told God she'd never get spanked in school again. Never ever. She would listen and watch for her turn to read and maybe win the Best Reader Award.

* * * * * * * * *

Next time she came awfully close to a spanking at home was when Alice Ann came up with the idea of a pretend birthday party. One day she just decided to tell everyone in Kindergarten that they were invited to the studio for a party after school on Friday. Parties were great fun. Jo Ann had had a party at her house where they all took presents and ate cake with ice cream and played "Button, Button" and blew up some balloons to try sitting on. There were paper streamers hanging from the ceiling and little horns to blow, and Mrs. Thompson didn't even care that lemonade got spilled on her rug.

She meant to tell them not to bring presents, but on Friday Lois and Honey Lou and Jo Ann and Wilma Jean all brought wrapped packages and walked home with Alice Ann. When they all walked into the studio together, Mother was surprised to hear about the party, even when Alice Ann said she would go up the street and around the corner to Swanson's Drug Store for ice cream. It didn't please Mother. She told the girls it was a big mistake, to go on home, and there wasn't going to be a party. She said it with frowny eyes and a real cross-looking mouth.

Alice Ann was surprised that Mother couldn't believe it had been a good idea. She knew for sure it hadn't been when Mother made her get ready for bed right then and there. In the middle of the afternoon! Even with the curtains pulled shut by her bed, Alice Ann couldn't go to sleep. She wasn't tired at all. There were too many sounds going on, like children down the street playing kick-ball, and Customers coming in and out of the studio, getting their pictures and leaving films to be developed. Nobody came near. Not even Ned came to look at her in bed. Daddy peeked in once and shook his head. Nobody cared about her. She'd probably *never* have a birthday party. Even when she got to be six there wouldn't be balloons and "Button, Button" and ice cream and presents. At school on Monday the girls would look at her and laugh. Here she was, thinking-about-it-long-and-hard, without Mother even having to tell her to. A spanking would be over and done, but the thinking about it would go on and on, at least until after supper, which might not happen for her there in her bed.

* * * * * * * * * *

Looking back, Alice Ann decided that her very most favorite grown-up in the whole world was Helen. Mother said that Helen had been there from the day Alice Ann came alive. "Helen-was-in-the-room-beside-Doctor-Amick-and-Grandma-when-you-were-born." Mother always said things fast so that you really had to listen. It was just her way. Helen didn't talk fast. She got down beside you and put her arm around you and spoke like she was telling you an awfully good secret between just the two of you. Helen made you feel special, like you could understand all the big words she used.

Helen had been a teacher right alongside Mother in the Elementary Building; that's what Helen called it. Mother just said "Grade School." When they were both just new marrieds, they walked to school and back together. When they got home, sometimes they fixed supper together for their husbands: Doc and Daddy.

Doc was a best friend, too. He didn't talk much, but he always smiled, and when he laughed his big, strong, happy laugh, he slapped his knee hard. Doc's job was to fix teeth in his office over the candy store. Alice Ann loved Doc, but he was still second to Daddy.

Helen smelled of flowery perfume all the time, different from Mother who always had the smell of cooking and cleaning and sometimes baby powder when Ned was first around. Helen had jars and bottles of fancy creamy stuff to put on her face that made the "Helen Smell." When Alice Ann was real little, she'd tiptoe into Helen's bathroom and shut the door. Then she'd sit on the closed-up toilet right next to the shelf where Helen kept a big mirror to hold. First was holding it and making all sorts of faces into it. Then came picking up one of the fancy jars that said "Helene" and something else she couldn't figure out how to say. Unscrewing the lid was easy and she'd never touch the goopy cream inside, but just smell it and then smell it again. It was the Helen smell. That wonderful Helen smell. It must be nice to have your name on jars where everyone would know they were yours, like Helen had.

Then Helen would call and say their tea-party was ready, so Alice Ann would put the jars back where they'd been and go drink tea with Helen out of real china cups. After Helen's baby Charles came along, Alice Ann was pretty sure the tea-parties would stop, but Helen just put the bassinet into the bathtub where little Charles couldn't be wakened by their giggling. Helen always seemed to have time for fun things, and it turned out to be wrong to brag about it to Ned, and Charles later on when they were big enough to be maybe a little bit jealous.

One day Ned said he had a secret about Helen and Doc. He wouldn't tell her until Alice Ann begged, and then she was sorry she'd wanted to know. "Helen and Doc have bottles of wicked whiskey in their Frigidaire, so there!" He said it whispery, and she didn't believe it for a minute, but next chance she got, she peeked inside. Sure enough, there were brown bottles all lined up on a shelf. They were like the ones left lying in the ditch beside the studio, called "dead soldiers" by the big boys going by. It was something to think about for a long time, but not ask anyone about. For sure, Helen didn't drink the wicked whiskey. Only Doc maybe would. And if he would, maybe, just maybe Helen would, too. The thinking about it was hard. Helen was still the next best thing to a mother. Now, though, there was a new, nice, kind of safe feeling with Mother, because Alice Ann knew she'd never have to worry about brown bottles being in their ice box. And Daddy would make sure of it. Still, it was a thing to think over and wonder about.

* * * * * * * * * * *

The studio's skylight filled up half of the Heavy Room's ceiling and also the north wall halfway down to ledges that were too high for Alice Ann to reach, dusting. The big glass frosted squares let light in even when the sun wasn't shining.

"North light is best for taking pictures," she heard Daddy tell a salesman once. She wondered why that was; it seemed to her that any light was best. When the sky outside was filled up with clouds and even rain, there was always enough light in the Heavy Room to see to color in her coloring books, lying there on her tummy next to the battleship green congoleum, spreading out the Crayola crayons in a neat row to choose from.

38

When a wedding party came to the studio straight from Saint Josaphat's Catholic Church with bouquets of flowers and organdy dresses to have wedding pictures taken, and there wasn't any sunshine and especially when it was raining, Daddy told them to go on over to the photographer in Grand Island. Once when that happened, the wedding people got real mad and stomped out calling him names. Even when Daddy explained that he only took photographs in "natchurlight," they said nasty things to him and Alice Ann was so embarrassed to hear it.

Daddy never used electric lights for taking pictures inside. He stood right up to people like the wedding, smiling all the time, but with the one side of his face twitching from the bomb shells exploding in the War Over There. It was easy to feel sorry for Daddy and for the wedding people; sorrier for Daddy not getting paid money that day; sorry for herself not getting to see the bride's long dress and smell the bridesmaids' perfume and talk to the little flower girl.

Once a salesman came bringing a big bunch of lights he called a "bank," on a metal stand for Daddy to try out. He said it was the latest thing and every photographer in the land had them. Well, it took Daddy a long time to even try them out and decide he wasn't happy with them. By that time the salesman phoned that it was too late to take them back, all paid for and everything. They stood in the corner for a long, long time and Alice Ann wondered if they would be there forever. She didn't say anything about it because Mother said it was a "sore point" with Daddy.

The day that the hail storm came and broke the skylight in the ceiling was a mixture of scaredness and sadness and hard to understand. Big pieces of glass fell all over the green congoleum, and Mother quick took Alice Ann around to the Ideal Cafe for an ice cream soda. She grabbed her handbag in one hand and Ned in the other and said, "Alice Ann-it's-way-too-danger-ous-to-be-in-the-studio-today."

It took a long time before all the glass pieces were swept up and the rain water mopped, so Ned and Alice Ann both got two ice cream sodas and came home through the back door. They could hear Harvey up on the studio roof, hammering wooden pieces to the place where the skylight ceiling had been. They would always be there, Daddy said, even if it made the Heavy Room darker now that there was ceiling all the way across and the "natchurlight" coming only from the window squares in the north wall.

Now they couldn't look straight up to see sunshine, but Daddy said it was a "sight safer," and he showed Alice Ann the jagged cuts in the green congoleum where glass had hit. She guessed she understood, but she wondered why they couldn't get stronger glass to put in the ceiling. Sometimes what grown-ups did and said was a puzzle, but "Daddy-knows-best" was one of the things Mother said a lot. And Daddy lots of times said, "Mother knows best." She wondered if there would ever be a time when they'd say, "Alice Ann knows best." An awful lot of learning would have to go on before that day, for sure.

Being the big sister was something she liked most of the time. It meant watching to see that Ned didn't take even one step into the alley where big trucks were always zooming out without even honking. It was then that Alice Ann would practice saying she knew best, but the older Ned got, the more he shook his head and said, "You're not the boss of me." Little brothers could be pests sometimes and friends most times.

The Saturday morning she was teaching Ned how to wipe the breakfast dishes was one time she almost didn't even like him. He wouldn't follow her directions and do it right. He would wipe the glasses on the outside, but never all the way inside. Even if she told him and told him the right way, that morning Ned just grinned a silly "I dare you" grin and wiped the next one his own way.

Suddenly, without thinking even, Alice Ann bopped him on his head with the milk bottle she'd just finished drying. Not a real hard bop. Just a little tap, really, but he turned around and screamed bloody murder and made tears come out of his squinted-up eyes. Sure then, Mother came running, and sure enough, Ned told. He stopped crying right away when Mother said, "All-right,-neither-of-you-goes-to-the-picture-show-this-afternoon." It was always something they did!

There was just no use arguing, once Mother made up her mind. Alice Ann begged and promised "never-never-again"; Ned started crying harder than before and said it hadn't hurt a bit. He was telling the truth, but it made no difference to Mother. They were both being punished and had to go outside while Mother finished up the dish-drying. Honey Lou came by on her way to the matinee at the Liberty like always, but the Conger kids couldn't go with her. Mother made that plain all over again. Ned and Alice Ann got big stirring spoons and dug holes to China by the hollyhocks in the backyard. Then they found ant holes to mash down and stomp on. When they got tired of that, they just sat in the swing and looked at each other, wishing it was back in the morning with the breakfast dishes still to be wiped.

* * * * * * * * * *

If she grew up to be beautiful, Alice Ann would join the "COLE BROTHERS CIRCUS COMING TO TOWN." She would wear pink silk stockings and red lipstick and a short "sticky-out" skirt like the lady on the poster they hung up on the studio's glass front door. Oh yes, she'd ride the white horse, too, the one with the big floppy feather tied onto its head. And before she did that, she'd hand out tickets to all the kids who couldn't pay to get into the circus.

For a long time she studied the poster, tracing the fancy letters and the picture of the Big Top tent with her fingers so she could draw it in her Big Red tablet. If she closed up her eyes, she could almost hear the circus music and smell the pop corn and know there wasn't enough money for her and Ned to go to the "COLE BROTHERS CIRCUS COMING TO TOWN."

"Alice-Ann-you'll-see-enough-of-the-circus-at-the-parade-down-Main-Street," Mother reminded her at breakfast. And sure enough, it was a swell parade with even two elephants swinging their trunks and clowns throwing candy. Ned said he'd be a clown if he grew up to be funny. Sitting there on the curb in front of Swanson's Drug Store, they both screamed along with the other kids when the organ grinder's monkey came close enough to spit at them. The trapeze people strutted past and turned somersaults while the lion tamer crackled his whip at the lion roaring like crazy in his cage. Balloons of every color were handed out, and she was glad that Ned got one.

All of a sudden there was a big red painted wagon pulled by two white horses. Alice Ann could see it was the end of the parade. The wagon stopped at the intersection, and Mr. Vodendahl from the lumber yard opened up the back end of the wagon. He began shoveling sand out into the street in piles, and he motioned for the kids

along the way to come jump into the sand. So they did ... the Gzhoviaks and the Wardyns and the McGhyhys and the Mendyks and the Congers. They slid and hopped around in the sand, and when Mendel Archerd sat down in it, he found the dime. He'd picked up some sand to throw and there was a shiny dime mixed in. Then another kid found a nickel, and they all started shouting and pushing and shoving and finding pennies mostly, but lots of them. Alice Ann tried to scoot Ned out of the way, since he wasn't as big as most, but he slid between somebody's legs and brought up a funny-looking wooden circle bigger than a quarter with writing on it. Before he could throw it back, she grabbed it and held onto it until they could get out of the sand. Everything was getting too wild and scary, she thought.

Anyway, Mr. Vodendahl started sweeping all the sand toward the curbs, and nobody was finding money any more. The parade was 'way off, heading to the empty lot by Jenners' Park where the tents were set up.

Most of the words printed on the wooden nickel were ones she could read; especially she knew: "GOOD FOR ONE FREE PASS AT COLE BROS. CIRCUS GATE." Her chest felt tight and happy at the same time. It was just the answer to a prayer. Then she remembered Ned had found it, so he should be the one to use it. Running home to show Mother, Alice Ann wished they'd found two.

Mother smiled at the good luck of having it, and she said something they both couldn't believe. "Ned-is-too-little-to-stay-up-as-late-as-the-circus-lasts-Alice-Ann-should-use-it." She wasn't sure that she'd heard right. Alice Ann waited for Mother to change her mind when she saw Ned's chin trembling so. But she didn't say anything more. Mother knew best. And just maybe she knew how hard Alice Ann had wished to go to the circus. The busting-out joy of it was almost too much to stand, like on Christmas morning when you couldn't open all the presents at once.

When Helen and Doc came by and heard the good luck, they said they'd take Alice Ann to the circus with them. And she could stay all night at their house, since they lived closer to the circus lot and it would be 'way too late and dark to walk the blocks back to the studio. The promise of it was almost too much to hold tight inside her chest, so tight there wasn't room inside her for salmon patties or corn or applesauce at supper.

It was all too exciting to even believe. But sure enough, there she was on the top row of the stands, with cotton candy all over her face and some even on her neck. The sights and sounds of the Cole Brothers Circus were all around her like a magic dream someone else was having. And the clean hankie in her pocket was fine to wipe off the sugary stuff. She didn't want to get it too dirty, since it was her fancy, not-washed-yet handkerchief with "Alice Ann" embroidered in loopy letters.

Not until they were walking back in the dark to Helen's and Doc's house did she discover the handkerchief was missing. How very horrible to have dropped it somewhere along the way or even back at the circus!

All the fun and excitement were crowded out of her with losing the Alice Ann hankie. It wasn't something you wanted to tell right away to anybody. She wanted to cry, but didn't. Tiredness came over the sadness almost before she was in bed, and sleeping covered all her worry for awhile. The dreaming that came was all about the circus and the Alice Ann hankie blowing in the wind like a banner over the circus center ring.

When she woke, it was still dark, but the birds were beginning their morning chirps, so she knew she'd slept enough. Pulling on her dress and socks, it was easy to tiptoe out of the bedroom, hearing Doc's loud snoring in the next room. Then out through the kitchen and living room and carefully through the front door. Alice Ann strapped on her shoes and ran down the street to the lot where the circus had been and now where they were taking down the big tent and folding up the wooden stands where the handkerchief just had to be, since it wasn't lying on the mashed-down grass going in.

It was all different looking now, with the sky above instead of tent cloth called canvas. There was only one set of seats still standing, and men were beginning to pull them apart. She had to tell them why she'd come back, and when she did they hopped down and began looking for the Alice Ann hankie. All they found, though, were flattened pop corn bags and cigar butts and a half-eaten candy bar.

Pretty soon she knew it was no use looking any-more, and they were all so sorry that the Alice Ann hankie was nowhere to be found.

Walking back to Helen and Doc's, she bent down and looked ever so carefully along the sidewalk they'd taken to the circus. No luck. It was hard to understand why Helen was so cross to her about going back to the circus grounds; grown-ups were so hard to explain things to. They were worried that she'd gone all by her-self. She'd not been by herself; there were all those nice men helping her look and shouting to each other: "Didja find the Alice Ann hankie yet?" On the way home, she sorted out all the things since Ned found the wooden nickel. She hoped somebody who found the lost hankie would know to bring it to the studio. She hoped Daddy would let her have the circus poster with the lady in pink when he took it down from the front door. She hoped Ned would ask her all about the animals at the circus. Another hope was that there wouldn't be pun-ishment for going off by herself so early to the circus grounds. She hoped there would be French toast for breakfast.

* * * * * * * * * *

Alice Ann knew that God wasn't in the big white globe in the ceiling of the Heavy Room. Anybody who could make a whole big world in only six days had to be bigger than anything, much bigger than a big, giant eye. God was able to do all sorts of miracles, and must be awfully busy with really more important things than sitting in a light bulb, no matter how big it was.

Mrs. Beuschausen in charge of Sunday School said God heard your prayers when you talked to Him at night on your knees. The only way for Ned to get a bicycle and then a paper route and then money to go to Boy Scout Camp was for God to do it. They didn't have enough money for even a used bike like the one Paul got by pulling weeds and picking up ground apples for Aunt Belle. Once in awhile Alice Ann got to hang out Aunt Belle's washing for a nickel a time. Aunt Belle wanted her underpants and petticoats hung at the back end close to the garage, where no one walking by could see them. It was hard to remember, and when she forgot, she only earned three pennies. Pennies added up, but very slowly.

Alice Ann told Ned she wasn't sure how God could handle getting a bicycle, but it seemed like the only way. To pray for it, that is. Every night, just before jumping into bed, they'd ask Him to please move the shiny red boy's bicycle out of Kaminski's Hardware Store window and into the studio where they lived. Ned wasn't so sure it could be done.

They didn't tell anyone about the prayers. When they were answered, it would be a really special miracle. Just supposing about how everyone would stand back in wonder and surprise was such fun, they'd sometimes forget to even pray about it. Most nights Alice Ann would remember; then she'd also promise not to pick off her scabs and never to hit Ned and always flush the toilet and tell the truth. They knew that God didn't like liars.

All the long summer she hoped and prayed and be-
haved. But nothing like the miracle happened. Together
with Ned, she'd saved $1.28 toward buying the red
Schwinn in Kaminski's window. The price on the tag
said: $11.00. Every time they walked to the meat mar-
ket, they would stop in front of the hardware store and
look. Ned stood so close that his breath made a little
wet circle on the glass. Alice Ann hoped that God was
looking down and could see how much they needed the
miracle. But no luck. It was so hard waiting.

On a day when school was almost ready to start,
Alice Ann and Ned were out in the street by the studio,
kicking Ned's football. They weren't out in the middle
where cars could hit them, but just alongside Aunt
Belle's driveway and roadside ditch, where the foot-
ball most often landed. Old dried-up leaves and dust
flew up when the ball came down into the ditch, and
Alice Ann said the next kick should be the last. Ned
booted it 'way up, and sure enough it landed in with all
the ditch's leaves. Running over and picking it up, she
screamed bloody murder. Right there, underneath the
football was a piece of green money, kind of crinkled
up and dirty. But *money*.

When Daddy smoothed out the money on his front
desk, he said that it wasn't a one-dollar bill, but a ten.
A TEN DOLLAR BILL! The *answer* to Alice Ann's
prayer! Ten whole dollars in one piece of money and
right there where they could find it! She wanted to yell
out: "THANK YOU, GOD! THANK YOU! But the look
on Daddy's face and his head shaking stopped her.

"Someone-lost-their-ten-dollars-in-Aunt-Belle's-
ditch." It was Mother saying it, coming quick to the
desk when she heard the commotion. Then Daddy said

the very same thing. He said that somebody was "out ten dollars." But Alice Ann wanted to yell that somebody was IN ten dollars and we're the somebody!

The why-it-was-there didn't seem like one of God's miracles to Daddy or Mother. Ten dollars could pay the rent or buy the month's groceries for a family.

It was more money than Alice Ann had ever seen. She and Ned each had a turn at holding it, but then Daddy pulled out the money drawer in his big desk and put the ten dollar bill safely under the lift-up change box. He smiled kind of sadly, and kind of sweet, too. He talked then about sure, it was a wonderful surprise and enough money for the bicycle for Ned, but it was maybe all the money someone had to last out the month. Grown-ups were so hard to understand when it came to money. She didn't even want to hear that a customer might come asking if they'd seen the ten dollar bill that was lost.

Daddy said, "We won't advertise that the ten dollars was found. There might be too many 'takers.' We'll keep it here for awhile to see if anybody inquires concerning it." Alice Ann didn't understand all that he said, except that they just couldn't run right down to Kaminski's Hardware for the bicycle. She knew then that the miracle from God was too good to be true.

Each time a customer came into the studio, Alice Ann held her breath, waiting for Mr. Bob Jenner or Mr. Louie Gzehoviak or Mrs. Alonzo Paige to come asking about the ten dollars. It was for sure a miracle, straight from God. All of the prayers they'd prayed every night had been answered. And in a way they'd never even imagined.

How long the money stayed in Daddy's drawer she

didn't know. Long after the County Fair was over and fourth grade started, Daddy decided maybe it had been long enough waiting. When he took out the miracle money, Alice Ann wondered if it might get spent for settling up the Meat Market bill or maybe for winter coats or the new kitchen stove they needed.

When none of the people walking by the studio every day came looking for the ten dollars, Daddy said perhaps the gypsies had dropped it. During the street carnival, they parked their wagons on the same side street where the studio sat. Then they told fortunes and sold magic rocks and beaded pillows. Neither Ned nor Alice Ann could play in the ditch or street when the gypsies were there. Helen said that was because sometimes gypsies stole children right out from under their folkses' noses. That was scary enough to make you stay inside looking out and wondering about being a gypsy child, riding all over the country and maybe never going to fourth grade at all.

On a beautiful fall day, Daddy and Ned went to Kaminski's and came home with a shiny Schwinn bike and Ned grinning from ear to ear. He couldn't have a paper route until February when he turned seven, but he could "sub" for Paul and learn how to be a paper boy. He said he'd let Alice Ann "sub" for him when he got to be a real paper boy and was sick. He'd for sure have money enough by next summer for Boy Scout Camp. Alice Ann was so very proud of him. It crossed her mind then to start praying for the miracle of Ned going to camp for sure.

She thought about it a long time, but decided maybe there were lots of other kids needing miracles. Her next prayer could be only a "thank you," not a "gimmee."

She thought that God might like to be thanked once in awhile.

"Alice-Ann-loves-her-little-brother." It was something she heard Mother say, never to her exactly, but always talking to someone else. It was hard to remember when it first started, and she never worried about why Mother said it. She wondered mostly why it needed to be said so many times. Mother said it to Helen and Doc, to Thelma and Harvey, to Dora and Bob Jenner, and to the Aunts. Once, Mother even said it to a customer in the studio, while Alice Ann was dusting the stair railing up to the frame room. "Oh, yes," Mother said, "Alice Ann loves her little brother."

What Mother said was true enough. It was hard not to love Ned. To begin with, he was what Grandmother C. called "a handsome little bit of heaven." When he was real little, Ned did look like one of the angels in a painting that Daddy framed and hung behind his big front desk, hoping someone would buy. Ned, until he was five, had a little curl right in the middle of his forehead, and big blue eyes like Daddy's, always looking at you ready with a question.

Ned's questions were always there; even when he was older and lots smarter, he would ask about everything. She didn't mind the questions. They were good ones like: "How does the ball know which way to bounce?" and "Does our alley out there go all the way through town and stop at the river?" Alice Ann made up answers if she wasn't sure, but ones that made him smile and think up another one. Sometimes it was easy to make up a story with the answer; once she made a poem right there on the spot. Ned really liked that and begged for another.

Ellen didn't love her brother Frank. She hated him; that is what she said. Alice Ann felt sorry for Ellen; it was the only thing she was sorry about Ellen. She had Dr. Amick for a daddy and they all lived in the biggest, nicest house in town, with a sunroom all made of windows and a real fireplace and a grand piano. Whenever you walked into their house, it smelled of cinnamon rolls fresh out of the oven. What fun it would be to live in Ellen's house. But it wouldn't be fun to live there with a brother like Frank.

Frank Amick was a real pest. He always followed them around, even when Ellen closed her bedroom door and locked it. Frank found another key and unlocked the door and squirted them with his squirt gun. He called Ellen "Fatso" and stuck out his tongue at Alice Ann. But the worst thing Frank did was to lock the playhouse door while Ellen and Alice Ann were inside. Then he went into his house and threw the key down the toilet. Frank told them through the window what he'd done with the key and went "Nyahh-nyahh-nyahh." It wasn't so much fun playing inside all locked in. Alice Ann thought she should be going home, so Ellen pushed open the playhouse side window and they crawled through it, skinning their knees on the rough window sill and tearing Ellen's dress.

Ned would never have done anything mean like that, Alice Ann knew for sure, but she didn't say it. She just felt sorry for Ellen having to put up with such a mean brother. Maybe he would change when he got to be older. He sure needed to.

When Ellen could come to play with Alice Ann at the studio, it had to be on a day when there wasn't a customer coming for a sitting. She didn't get there many times. When Ellen did, they found things to play with out in the sleeping porch, like Chinese Checkers and Hang-Man and jigsaw puzzles and paper dolls. But Ellen most times wanted to look through Daddy's camera to see Alice Ann upside down. When she sat down on the long storage bench that Mother covered with flowered creton, she rubbed her bottom and said, "Don't you have any soft benches?" In the bathroom, she tried turning on the other spigot, the one with "H" on it. Paul laughed at it not having hot water come out, and he said the "H" stood for "Heck, no."

"Wow, doesn't your house have hot water?" Ellen asked. Alice Ann knew she should tell the truth, but something made her say sure they did, just not in the bathroom. It was a lie, she guessed. A little one. The studio didn't have a hot water heater like the one in Ellen's basement. It made her face all hot to think about how some families not as rich as Ellen's used the tea kettle on the kitchen stove to get their hot water. Daddy heated water on the hot plate in the darkroom when he needed it. So they really *did* have hot water, just not all the time.

Once she'd said the lie, it couldn't be taken back. Alice Ann was sorry about that. She was even sorrier when Ned, who was listening, told Mother, "Alice Ann told a lie to Ellen." There was a worry about what the punishment would be for telling a fib. God might forgive her, but she wasn't so sure about Mother. The wondering went on a long time while she waited, getting ready to have her mouth washed out with soap, or maybe something worse. Nothing happened. Ned told it again at supper. Nothing happened then. Everybody just kept on eating. Ned was a big blabber mouth; she told him so that night before prayers. Somehow, she still loved him. Ned was really that hard not to love.

* * * * * * * * * * *

By the time Ned was old enough to climb all of the steps to the landing that led to Daddy's frame-making room, Alice Ann was even tall enough to see over the top of the wooden stair rail alongside, and down into the Heavy Room where photographs were taken. Also, she could see into the far corner where their living room alcove was. Mother called it that, an alcove where the davenport that opened up into a bed was, and the radio and big floor lamp. Its ceiling was as high as the Heavy Room's, but there were walls to separate it from where the customers sat to be photographed.

Standing high up on the stairs you could watch people coming through the front door, but Daddy's big desk was hidden by a partition (that was another neat grown-up word she liked).

If no business was going on to see down below, Ned and Alice Ann sat on the high up landing with the Toy Town spread out to play with and wait to hear what went on down below. The stair bannister was solid wood, so nobody could know the two of them were there, that is, until Mother came looking.

On the day of the Kowalski wedding pictures, Mother was way too busy ironing the bride's veil and wrinkles out of the flower girls' dresses. When they first heard the wedding bunch come tromping in, Ned's mouth made a big "O," but Alice Ann put her finger up to her lips for him to keep still. Then she smiled a kind of signal to let him know that it was like their secret to be hiding up there where nobody could see or hear them.

Mother and Daddy didn't like for the photographer's

54

kids to be hanging around anytime pictures were being taken. Alice Ann was pretty sure that it was getting too late to come walking down the steps, especially when she heard Daddy talking to Mr. Kowalski. She wished she could've seen Daddy's face when another man said real loud, "AW, C'MON, STUB! A LI'L OL' DRINK WILL DO YOU GOOD!"

A kind of sweetish but rotten smell came floating up to where Alice Ann and Ned sat. Then they heard a lady's voice, telling that it was no use to offer Mr. Conger whiskey because he was a teetotaler, whatever that meant. Well, sometimes he drank tea with Mother, so that must be what the lady meant.

There were sounds of people coming into the Heavy Room and rustling organdy dresses and laughter; somebody told a joke and they all laughed. A flower girl couldn't find her flower basket. Ned wanted to stand up and look, but Alice Ann wouldn't let him do it. It would give away their hiding place if anyone looked up and saw Ned peeking over the bannister. They could hear Daddy moving his big portrait camera into place, and Alice Ann imagined him turning the wheel on the side that anchored it to one position. Then he was giving instructions: "Tip the chin up, Missus" and "Straighten the left shoulder, Alex" and "Now, smile, everybody."

What happened next was kind of funny. Right in the middle of all the quiet there was a loud, kind of silly lady-voice giggling and words coming out, "Hey, Mr. Conger, looky here! I'll show my fancy garter in th' pitchur!"

Together, like one person, Ned and Alice Ann popped their heads up over the bannister and leaned down to

see. They must've made some noise, knocking over the Toy Town that started rolling down the steps, because the next thing they saw was the whole bunch of wedding people looking up at them. Even Daddy came out from under the black cover-up cloth. Then all of a sudden Mother was running up the stairs with a very cross-looking face.

It took forever to pick up all the Toy Town pieces that tumbled down, but Mother waited and Daddy waited and the wedding people waited. A bridesmaid was throwing up in the bathroom or they would've had to go sit there for an hour. Instead, they went to the backyard to sit on a bench and "think-about-it." They never did get to see the bride's fancy garter.

KNOWING THAT NOTHING STAYS THE SAME

She guessed that she'd been photographed at least one hundred times, posing in front of the painted background that covered most of the wall. Alice Ann must've looked into the glass eye of the camera's lens more than anybody in town had, reading the "Keep Smiling" sign just above, and turning the corners of her mouth up into a kind of pasted-on happy look. Being the Photographer's Daughter was good most always, she decided, sitting there while Daddy hid under the black cloth, waiting for his hand to pop out from under, to squeeze the bulb that somehow told the camera to take a picture.

It was for sure that all the girls in fourth grade had wished they belonged to the Photographer that day of Alice Ann's birthday party. After the ice cream, all 22 of them lined up family-group style there in front of the background and had a birthday-group photograph taken. Some days after, each girl got to have what Mother called a souvenir from the party: a 4 x 6 enlargement reminder in go-to-party dresses.

For Alice Ann's party there had been invitations with Indians and tomahawks. Mother made two brown paper Indian tepees, big enough for Ned and Charles to sit in the openings, dressed and painted like Apache warriors and handing out the prizes for the games they played. All sorts of games that Mother made up. Then was the opening of presents and birthday cake and lemonade. Maybe it was the lemonade that caused the funny, "floaty" and almost "sicky" feeling in her stomach, but also it might have been all the happiness she felt. What a strange thing, to be happy and kind of sick at the same time, wondering if she could keep from throwing up until everybody went home.

It was for sure a day to remember. The birthday group picture would always be there to remind her, alongside the "Happy Birthday" cards and the birthday party napkin she put in the big scrapbook that was Jo Ann's present. When she was an old, old lady, Alice Ann would take out the scrapbook, look at Jacqueline's crooked teeth and Virginia's natural-curly hair and Doris Rowe's crossed eyes and, of course, her own face covered with freckles.

A few days afterwards, Daddy and Mother posed her and Ned standing beside the baby bed that Mother called a "bassinet," looking down at Alice Ann's biggest doll in a blanket, and it made them wonder the "why" of it. There they were, all fancy in Sunday School clothes with Alice Ann wearing the lace-up boots she loved. When the photograph was developed and printed, the boots didn't show, but sure as anything the two of them looked for all the world like they were seeing a baby in the bed. Mother put on her real smiley face and told them the picture was for something called "announcements." Mother said that pretty soon Ned and Alice Ann would have a baby brother or sister, whichever God decided.

The first thing to wonder about was why God had decided to have a baby come live with them. They already had a boy and a girl for their family. Why did they need another one that didn't even tell which it would be?

Mother looked happy about the baby coming. It was hard to tell if Daddy was the same. There were so many questions Alice Ann wanted to ask, but something told her not to, just then. It was a big happening to think about and talk about later. She knew that Helen would answer any question she asked her, but maybe it was still kind of a secret for only family to know.

Ned already knew that the baby would be a boy, because he needed a brother. That was a thing to worry about. Maybe another brother wouldn't be like Ned. What if he turned out just like Ellen's Frank? Somebody easy to hate. Every night after God-blesses, she told God that a sister would be much, much better. She promised to love a sister and take care of her when Mother was busy at the studio's front desk.

It seemed a long time before the baby sister came, just like she'd prayed for. It was worth thanking God two nights in a row. The name for the baby was Jane Ellen, and the day Alice Ann got to go see her at the hospital was the coldest day of the whole winter. Snow was piled up high all over town. It was like walking through a snow tunnel on the sidewalk past Helen's Dress Shop and the Legion Hall and Vodendahls' Hardware.

Carrying the baby rattle from Gdanitz's 5 and 10 and climbing the hospital stairs, you could smell all kinds of different smells: medicine and furniture polish and lye soap and wet diapers hanging up to dry on lines stretched across the stairs. Down the hall where Mother was sleeping in a bed, there was no baby. A stiff, frowny nurse came along and said that Jane Ellen was sleeping, too, and shouldn't have visitors. Alice Ann wanted to say back in a frowny, grown-up way, "I'm *not* a visitor! I'm a ***big sister!***" But she had to smile and let the stiff nurse walk her back downstairs to the front door. She still held the sack with the baby rattle, all wrapped in pink baby paper.

It was sad walking all the way back to the studio in the deep snow. To feel better, she thought how very little a new baby's hands were, too little to hold a rattle maybe. There would be lots of pictures taken of Baby Jane Ellen; maybe the rattle could be in a picture. Maybe Alice Ann could even sit in the photo, holding Baby Jane Ellen, and boy, would she smile!

Sometimes she couldn't make a smile come, no matter how hard she'd try and make believe she wasn't mad or sad. Being sick was not to smile about, for sure.

Elva Miller came to school smiling with the measles and she said she felt fine, just pretending, since she didn't want to miss the big kids' play that day in the Music Room. Elva looked fine with her nice red cheeks, like a movie star, but the red went down all over Elva's neck and arms.

Mr. Reynolds sent her home quick. You could hear her all the way up the stairs saying she felt fine, while the big kids' operetta was beginning. Alice Ann was sorry that Elva didn't get to see Hansel and Gretel shove the wicked witch into the oven. Later on, most of the boys and girls sitting in Elva's row that day came down with measles, including Alice Ann.

Being sick gave you a good excuse not to keep smiling. Measles were nothing to be happy about. She felt like pulling pictures off the wall and stomping on them. The itching was the worst, even in your hair. She couldn't wait to get over them and start smiling again. Nothing seemed right even the day the measles were gone. There was still something to make you frown and talk cross and kick the wheels of Jane Ellen's buggy. Why was *that?* Maybe since the buggy was always in the way when they wanted to set out the Toy Town with streets for Ned's cars to run on. Sure as anything, there would be Mother moving the buggy right in their play space, closer to the stove so Jane Ellen would be warm enough. That's when smiles didn't come and frowns were all Alice Ann could manage.

Babies were cute. Jane Ellen was the cutest baby they'd ever seen. Helen and Doc said so, too, oohing over the blond curls and big blue eyes just like Daddy's. She had dimples in her cheeks, just like Shirley Temple's. Alice Ann didn't have dimples. In the bathroom, she took the fingernail scissors out and pushed the sharp ends into her own cheeks, one at a time, holding until it hurt and before the skin bled. There! Sure enough, she had pokey-kind of dimples for a few minutes, but they didn't stay. Maybe if she did it every day, they would. But it was really too much trouble and felt sore.

"Alice Ann-I-know-what-we'll-do-to-make-you-curly-hair-like-Shirley-Temple's." She said it, combing Alice Ann's hair, to make nice curls and wrap rags around to hold them. Then there were long red curls like sausages for at least half a day. The curl just wouldn't stay in any longer, kind of like the trying dimples. It was then that Alice Ann decided what the Keep Smiling sign on Daddy's camera meant: smile to look your best for the picture-taking, not for all the time.

One of the things about growing up was your not feeling extra special all of the time. Maybe that was why grown-up people got frowny and cross and wrinkly and old. Not special. But Alice Ann needed to feel special again. When she'd had the measles, Mother read to her out of Book House Number Five, and put a cool cloth on her head and called her "precious." Now since God was so good at answering prayers, Alice Ann was tempted to pray for something to happen to her to make her feel special again. Not the measles. Maybe a broken arm like Jo Ann's when she fell out of the apple tree. Doctor Amick put a hard cast on it, and everybody wrote their names on it. They did nice things for her, and Jo Ann had a very good time with her broken arm, she told Alice Ann. She said she'd even do it again if she got the chance.

Well, what do you know? Alice Ann tripped going up the Public Library steps and clobbered her right leg. It was hard to walk, even. The big purple thing called a "bruise" ached much longer than Alice Ann had prayed for; she got to sit in Daddy's big chair and have both hot and cold cloths on the hurting. She even got to have cocoa in one of the company cups. Helen and Doc brought a bottle of keen-smelling lotion to put on her leg. She was beginning to feel like smiling again, but before she knew it, the specialness was over.

Everybody was worried about Jane Ellen maybe having something in her chest called "the croup." Mother said, "Alice Ann, it's-time-you-were-up-and-about-again." The leg still kind of hurt, especially when Alice Ann pushed on the bruise. Mother said, "Hurting-means-healing," whatever *that* meant, and told her

62

to go warm Jane Ellen's bottle in the pan on the stove. They all just didn't care that her leg might even be broken! Well, maybe it wasn't, since she could walk on it. So one day, she found Daddy's hammer in the storage closet, gritted her teeth, and pounded with the hammer on the bruise until it hurt some more. She really couldn't walk very well. When Dr. Wanek took a look, he said well, maybe there was a little bone chip inside, but not to worry, it wasn't "going anywhere."

Figuring out how to make something else go wrong with her leg was too hard. The thing to do, she decided, was to pray again, explaining to God that she loved Jane Ellen a lot, and she knew babies needed lots of people's time. But *Alice Ann* needed some, too. She wished for a Keep Smiling Day with lots of happiness. Was that too much to ask? A broken arm like Jo Ann's might be the answer. And she hadn't had the mumps yet, like Paul. There was a girl at Catholic School who fell into hot ashes and got burned. That was maybe too much. Alice Ann would leave it up to God. Maybe there was another way for her to feel special. She loved all the Get Well cards that came with having measles. But people didn't get measles twice, Mother said.

"Alice Ann-just-isn't-herself-today," Mother would say sometimes. When she was little, Alice Ann wondered what that meant. It was easy to imagine herself being someone else, maybe like Thelma with red-painted toenails and a Marcel in her hair and lipstick and eyebrows that were painted on. God sure couldn't manage that. But she'd leave it up to Him. And while He was in the business, could he manage to give her some curly hair, like Shirley Temple's?

Another thing Mother said a lot was "It's-not-a-good-day-to-go-asking-friends-over-to-play." She said it in her Mother-knows-best voice that meant it was no use begging. Way down deep, Alice Ann wanted to live in a real house, not the studio, but she didn't dare tell even Ned. Even sometimes on a cloudy day when she knew Daddy wouldn't be taking portraits, Mother wouldn't let other kids come in and play.

Then Alice Ann and Ned would roller-skate up the sidewalk to the corner, being careful not to skate into Aunt Belle's bushes. They were *really* Uncle Ashley's, after all. He did the planting and watering and trimming. But it was always Aunt Belle looking out her window at them skating, to see if one of them was too close to the bushes. Spirea grew all the way up to the corner, and it started close beside the studio whose wall was the divider line of something called "property." If Alice Ann put her hand out the kitchen window, it was on Aunt Belle's and Uncle Ashley's property.

Aunt Belle's face was like in the funny papers: little beady eyes and squished-up mouth and frizzy hair dyed red with a toothbrush dipped in red ink. She was nicely round and fat, but she frowned a lot. Mother said, "It's-best-to-keep-the-peace-with-Aunt-Belle," whatever that meant. So it was a fine surprise when Mother stood right up to Aunt Belle, telling her that Alice Ann and Ned had *not* broken that bush with their wagon like Aunt Belle said. She put her hands on her hips and said right to Aunt Belle's face that she was mistaken.

It was the very best thing that happened all that week, telling that *her* children didn't lie about things that important. Such a warm feeling came over Alice Ann, like a blanket on top of you on a cold night. It was good to know that Mother believed them, even enough maybe not to keep the peace, whatever that meant. Aunt Belle turned around real fast and stomped home, saying things under her breath. Ned and Alice Ann felt so good, to be trusted, even if you were just a kid. They made up their minds not to ever lie, even about little things like taking the last cookie or not flushing the toi-  let or picking your scabs. Grown-ups could somehow always know when you were lying.

You knew that there were kids who lied all the time. The McGhyhys were the very best at it. Richard and Jacqueline told lies so many times that it was hard to know when they told the truth. Oh, they could stand before Mrs. McGhyhy and tell lies, right into her face, like swearing it wasn't them who stole the peaches off Whartons' tree. Alice Ann wondered if sometimes they believed their own lies, like having baby kittens under their front porch.

As far as Ned and Alice Ann could tell, there weren't any kittens where Jacqueline said. They got Daddy's big rake and scooped out dirt and old newspaper, dog poop from underneath the porch, hoping to find kittens. Jacqueline said yessir, they were just too far back;

then she started crying. They wanted to believe her, really they did, since Jacqueline had bragged about it and told Alice Ann she could have one of the babies.

Much as anything, Alice Ann wanted to have a house to live in with a porch where baby kittens could hide for you to find. She wished like everything to live in a real house where you could yell out loud if you wanted to, and really cry when you bumped your head and have friends come over any old time. She knew way down deep that she shouldn't even tell Ned how much she wanted it, making her worry that maybe it was a *lie* to pretend that she was happy living in the studio. Well, God had answered some of her prayers. Maybe she could ask God to do something about it. God was someone you didn't have to smile and pretend with.

All sorts of really good things would happen when Daddy's "ship came in." Mother would get a new stove. They'd have a frigidaire instead of an ice box. Daddy would have a car like Doc and Helen's. Before she knew better Alice Ann thought a ship would someday come sailing up the Loup River, all loaded with surprises and a flag on it saying the ship was all for the Conger family.

Daddy laughed sometimes and said things would get better when his "ship came in." But he didn't mean a real live ship. It was kind of a dream of Daddy's, that might never come true.

Then there was the day she carried the contest entry to the newspaper office, praying for Daddy to win and get the big money that was promised. It was almost a sure thing; hadn't he spent hours upstairs working on the contest, where you had to count the white dots in a black box printed on a page of the *Loup City*

66

Leader? Mother said, too, that Daddy was an expert at things like contests. He had a "system," whatever that meant, carefully blacking out each white dot and then making a mark on paper for each dot. Alice Ann was sure that nobody else could've thought to do such a wise thing.

Twelve o'clock noon on Friday was what the paper called a deadline. At ten minutes 'til, Alice Ann stood at the basement door of the *Leader* office with Daddy's contest entry in an envelope and the silver dollar fee tied up in her hankie. But the door was locked! She couldn't imagine why; it was the only way to get into the newspaper office. Her loud knock brought a man to the door, and he opened it just wide enough to say, "Go home, little girl." No, not for nothing would she go home! She told him so in a trembly kind of voice. Alice Ann said it wasn't twelve o'clock yet, since the noon whistle hadn't blown, and she had her daddy's contest entry right here with the dollar fee. When the man said it was too late anyway, she wanted to scream at him, but he shut the door quick and locked it. Leaning against the door's window, she pounded again to get in, but the man along with others just kept packing up boxes and tying them shut.

Crying wouldn't help, Alice Ann knew. But suddenly tears pushed out of her eyes so that she couldn't see straight and tripped going up the basement steps. Alice Ann was sure that Daddy's was the very entry to win. Did that man suspect it, too, and not want him to win? Why else would he shut the door in her face? Was it because she was just a little girl? Should Daddy maybe have brought the entry to the newspaper office himself? That man would *not* have told Daddy to go home.

That's just what she said when she got back to the studio. Mother's face was almost as sad as Alice Ann's. Daddy just laughed and said, "Well, we didn't waste a dollar after all." Later, Daddy told that it was all over town that the contest had been a scam, whatever that meant. Police Chief Oscar said the men had taken all the entry money and skipped out of town. Alice Ann thought of the long time Daddy had spent, covering the dots and counting them; she dug the worked-on paper out of the waste basket, smoothed it out, and folded it up to save in her treasure pencil box. It just seemed the right thing to do.

The very minute Thanksgiving Day dishes were put away, Ned and Alice Ann started counting the days. They took down the kitchen calendar from its hook and added up the days left in November and those in December up to Number Twenty-Five. It wasn't that hard for Ned; he was a smart little kid for a second grader.

All that Ned wanted for Christmas was a train set just like the one in Vodendahl's Hardware. He wrote his own letter to Santa Claus, listing each of the railroad cars he especially wanted, doing good with the spelling. Alice Ann helped him look up "caboose" in Daddy's fat dictionary.

"Now-Alice-Ann-you-must-write-your-letter-too," Mother reminded her while Ned put his letter into the envelope and addressed it to the North Pole. Now here was the big trouble, because this Christmas Alice Ann didn't believe. Oh, she could pretend for Ned when his eyes kind of sparkled whenever he talked about the sleigh and the reindeer and big pack of toys, like in "A Visit from Saint Nicholas." But this year she knew what everybody in fourth grade knew.

Knowing left a big, cold lump in her throat; one of the awful things about getting bigger and older was knowing things you honestly didn't want to know: where babies really came from, wars happening, Wilma Jean's daddy just walking out, no Easter Bunny hiding the eggs, and especially no reindeer up on the roof on Christmas Eve.

Alice Ann remembered asking Mother long ago, last year, about Santa Claus and what she said, "I've-never-seen-Santa" with a kind of tight smile that meant don't ask anymore about it. Alice Ann wanted to tell her right out loud that she'd never seen God, but she believed in Him. Maybe when she was eleven she'd be brave enough to say it. But that time she wanted to know for sure, so she had asked Daddy if there really was. It seemed a long, long time before he said anything. He was at the big front desk out in front, and she was dusting the steps to the frame-making room, but they were close enough for her to hear him adding up numbers and licking the pencil end.

While she waited, Alice Ann dusted the very corners of each step. She would always remember the smell of furniture polish on her cloth and dust balls flying up and seeing the worn places in the middle of each step where Daddy's feet walked every day. In her mind, she floated up over the stairway, like a Peter Pan, and looked down on Daddy's head bent over the cash book, fingers riding the columns down the page.

In a few minutes he cleared his throat, and she needed to lean over the wooden railing to hear exactly what he said. Even then the words were soft and kind of mumbled, but they were: "No, Alice Ann, there isn't." How strange for her to want to hear the words and not want to at the same time. She kept on dusting until the steps were cleaner than they'd ever been. Then she got the Spiegel catalog and found the page with all the Shirley Temple dolls. She carefully copied the price and the catalog number. Then she wrote her letter to Santa Claus and put it in an envelope and gave it to Daddy to mail, like always.

That Christmas Grandpa C. came to spend it with them, and he got to sleep in Alice Ann's bed. Mother made up the day-bed in the Heavy Room for Alice Ann to sleep in Christmas Eve, after Grandpa C. came on the bus. It was fun to stay up late with Grandpa C., having pop corn and cocoa and putting presents all around the little tree from out of the front window where it had stood all through December. Daddy was still putting photos in folders, but when the last customer had picked up Christmas present pictures, they locked the door and turned out the lights and went to bed.

Alice Ann made up her mind to stay awake there on the day-bed, but she had to keep pinching herself and making up poems to stay awake. Once she kind of dozed off and woke to hear Mother bringing a big chair to put up close to the day-bed. Lying still with her eyes shut was so hard. She took long, loud breaths when someone, Mother or Daddy, came to look at her. Then they went away and over to the Christmas tree where Alice Ann could watch them.

Daddy and Mother brought out some boxes and sacks of candy. They filled Ned's and Alice Ann's and Baby Jane Ellen's stockings, whispering and laughing quiet-like. She couldn't hear what they said, but smiled to herself seeing Daddy put train tracks together in the faint light from the Christmas tree. She could only watch through the slats in the chair beside her, but it was such fun to see your parents doing something together without knowing you are watching. She kind of wanted to get up and help. Seeing what she saw was something Alice Ann could never tell anyone, not in a million years. It was a secret to keep forever.

Alice Ann waited a long time after Mother and Daddy went to their bedroom. Then she got up to take a look at everything under the tree. Its light were off, so she had to see with only moonlight coming in the skylight windows. She only looked at things for her: a dear little wooden high chair for her Nancy Bell to sit in and a shiny round suitcase for doll clothes, some books and new bedroom slippers, all for her, she knew. But *no* Shirley Temple doll. She should have known. They were too expensive, even if the only thing she wanted. Going back to sleep was easy, and she dreamed about Ned seeing the train first thing in the morning. All of a sudden there he was in real life, tugging at her covers and yelling to come look, come look.

The Christmas tree lights were on again, and all the presents looked different in the bright morning light. Still, Alice Ann's feet dragged a little going to where Ned was still yelling while he ran his train. Like before, there was the doll high chair and the suitcase and books — and wait — THERE WAS THE SHIRLEY TEMPLE DOLL in plain sight where it hadn't been the night before! Mother was coming over and smiling and saying ever so quietly, "Alice Ann-nobody-should-cry-Christmas-morning."

* * * * * * * * * *

"Alice Ann-be-sure-to-wear-your-snow-pants-to-school-it's-much-too-cold-to-be-without-them." It was so hard for her to think of Mother ever being a little girl. She knew that all the grown-up ladies had been babies once and then little girls who turned into big ones. But even when she tried, Alice Ann could only think of Mother talking like a mother and frowning like a mother and smiling at Jane Ellen when she rocked her in a mother way.

It was hard to use her "imagination" like Miss Nichols said to in fourth grade when they wrote poems. Mother really had been going-on-eleven once, like Alice Ann. She'd even had a best friend who could never come over and play. Once Mother told how they would walk together from school past a long picket fence on the way to Opal's house first. They would each have a stick and would hit the fence pieces. With each hit they'd say together: "She won't! She won't! She won't!" hoping like everything that their saying it would make Opal's mother say "yes" just this once. She never did. Mother's best friend got sick and died before she even got to be in fifth grade. And Mother never had a best friend again. Not until she was a grown-up lady and was a teacher and found Helen.

Lois asked Alice Ann: "Am *I* your best friend?" Alice Ann thought a minute and told her "yes." Jo Ann asked her: "Am *I* your best friend?" Alice Ann thought two minutes that time and said, "Yes." Honey Lou asked her the same thing. It was easy to say "yes" by that time. Virginia never asked. Alice Ann wished she would. She wanted to have as many best friends as she could. That way, there wouldn't be any chance of her best friend dying before fifth grade. It was something to think about. Because old grandmas weren't always the only people who died.

Jo Ann heard about Alice Ann's other three best friends. On the way home from school she punched Alice Ann very hard and yelled at her: "You said *I* was your best friend!" It was kind of hard to explain to Jo Ann the reason for wanting more than one best friend. She just kept walking and Billy Hancock ran alongside, sticking his tongue out at Alice Ann. Then he stood in front of her and blocked the way while Jo Ann caught up with them and punched Alice Ann again. It was something that she didn't want to do especially, but Alice Ann pushed out both hands and shoved Jo Ann into the ditch they were standing by.

By that time she knew she should run home fast and she did, going faster than she ever remembered running, with Billy running right behind, yelling that he'd get his dad's shotgun and shoot her. Mr. Hancock was the sheriff, so he had a shotgun for sure.

Alice Ann got inside the studio door and told Daddy what had happened, except for the part about trying to have more than just one best friend. So Daddy walked back to where Jo Ann was and found out she wasn't hurt; but he brought Jo Ann back to the studio for Alice Ann to say she was sorry. She truly was. It was hard to know why she'd pushed Jo Ann by then. So, to make Jo

Ann feel better, she whispered in her ear, "You're my VERY best, SPECIAL friend of all." Even with Jo Ann's punches and Alice Ann's pushing, it was true. Maybe Honey Lou and Lois wouldn't mind being number two and number three. And it was still important to have more than one best friend.

It was Jo Ann she chose then, that day she was sick in school and Miss Nichols told her to pick someone to walk Alice Ann the six blocks home. She guessed she *was* kind of sick when it was so hard to keep the words on the blackboard from wiggling, and nothing around her seemed real and her head kept lying down on her desk.

Jo Ann did her best to help Alice Ann get her snow pants on sitting there in the hall, but her legs were too tired to hold up for it; Jo Ann said to just carry them. Snow was coming down and piling up all over everything, even getting down inside their overshoes. Jo Ann kept saying it was a real blizzard for sure. It wasn't easy to talk to each other because the wind kept blowing their words away and trying to pull apart their hands from holding to each other tight. Alice Ann felt kind of warm, but Jo Ann said it was the fever making her feel that way. Maybe it was the fever that made her eyes droopy and her chest too tight to breathe. Opening her mouth helped to get breath inside, and snowflakes on her tongue were like eentsy sugar cubes.

They walked a long way before Jo Ann said she had to go back to school, and could Alice Ann go by herself the last two blocks?

Snow had been shoveled into a skinny pathway past the courthouse, so then it was easier to walk. The studio was in the next block down, clear to the end. Alice

Ann turned to wave to Jo Ann and somehow got mixed up about which way to go, so Jo Ann came back and pushed her the other way toward home. Still, it was hard to walk through the snow, so when she came to a big pushed-up pile of it, Alice Ann sat down and with her bottom kind of carved out a seat to rest on. She could stay for just a little while to watch the snowflakes blowing around and across her face. It might be too much work to walk the rest of the way. Maybe she'd sit there until the snow stopped and somebody came to shovel a better path to the studio.

It was warm and toasty sitting there, but maybe

Mother wouldn't think it was such a good idea. Where was Mother, anyway? Why wasn't she there to help getting home? Maybe it would be better to stand up and walk instead of sitting. Maybe she could stand and join up with all the snowflakes flying. Why, that's just what she'd do! It would be so easy to float up there into the snowy sky and let Old Mr. North Wind sweep you on back to the studio.

So Alice Ann did it. Why hadn't she thought of it back at school? It was so much fun gliding along on the wind, watching downtown Loup City sitting there in the middle of a blizzard. Not too many people walking there. Really, not any. There were all safe in their houses. Just like Alice Ann would be soon.

In a little while there she was at the front door, knocking on the glass to let Mother know she had come home like she knew she should. But no one came and Alice Ann figured maybe she would need to go through the alley and around to the back door. The big problem was with her hands in the wet mittens. It was like she didn't have fingers anymore to work the knob on the studio's big front door.

It was about the time she'd decided to fly up into the snowstorm again and fly around, when Mother came hurrying and wiping her hands on her apron and looking worried. She took Alice Ann inside right away and into the bathtub. In the middle of the day! It felt good and she tried to wash her eyes so they would feel clean and warm and not filled up with cotton.

When she was tucked into bed, Dr. Amick was all of a sudden there beside her, taking her temperature and listening to her chest and making tsk-tsk sounds all the while. Alice Ann told him about sitting in the snowpile by the courthouse and maybe leaving her snowpants there. Dr. Amick said the strangest thing then: "Alice Ann, I could throw you out into the deepest snowbank in town and you wouldn't get any sicker than you are now." His voice seemed far away and his face faded into the wallpaper, and she felt too tired to think about it. Much better to close her eyes and sleep a little bit.

The dreams that came were trouble. It was so hard to tell them apart from what was really happening.

Nobody around her had faces, and the clock ticked too loud. The wind seemed to be blowing inside her chest, but then it was the clock beating inside, "tickety-tock-tickety-tock." Just like Alice in Wonderland, she felt "curiouser and curiouser," floating into and out of dreams and wanting something to drink, but not having the right words to say so. She tried like everything to tell Mother, but she'd turned into a frowny nurse with lipstick. Mother never wore lips ... Alice Ann tried to say, but it always came out "lips ... lips ... lipsick." She couldn't talk straight or even see straight. And one thing for sure, this bed wasn't hers anymore. Everything was so different — the smells, the sounds, the whole feeling of being somewhere special, but maybe only in a dream. It was *INSIDE A SUBMARINE,* of all things! Kind of dark and metal-smelling and a soft kind of machine thumping that never stopped, just kept on ka-lump-ka-lumping along in a kind of tune keeping time with her heart.

Alice Ann's whole body felt different, almost divided up into two parts: half in one room and the bottom half in some other place. Sure as anything, her head and arms and chest were lying inside a little room with a nice window all the way across. Through the window she could see her tummy and legs were all covered up with white paper. Trying to sit up to see better made a kind-looking Chinaman reach inside her first room and gently push her back onto the pillow. He smiled and gave her a curvy glass straw to drink with after the blue pills. Oh, the pills came so often she could imagine how they were all piled up inside her tummy, red and blue and green stacks.

The Chinaman had to come in from a hole in the

ceiling, she decided; he must use the ladder, crawling down into her room inside the submarine. Then Mother was there, smiling and patting her hand when Alice Ann told her how very nice the Chinaman had been. Pretty soon Daddy came, bringing the little ivory-handled fingernail scissors to trim her fingernails real short. It seemed like every time she looked up, there he was, smiling with his mouth but not his eyes and taking her hand in his to trim Alice Ann's fingernails 'way down until they almost hurt.

Maybe it was part of the dreaming, but when she pulled her hand away, he lifted it up to her face where now there were sores and bleeding from her scratching them. Blood came off on her hand, and she smeared it onto the window in front of her. It was a soft window, not made of glass like in Doc's car; the dream made her in a wrecked car, not a submarine, and there was blood on the windshield in front of her. Had she been in an accident? Places on her head hurt where she pulled off the scabs and inside her ears the same thing. Alice Ann tried not to pick off the scabs, but they itched and needed to be somewhere else in her dream, or was it a dream?

There was Mother talking through the window, saying they were in the new hospital and Alice Ann was one of the first people to be in it. Trying to understand made hurting inside her head, and she was too tired to listen and understand, so it was easy to close her eyes and her ears and try to get back into a dream about being home in her own bed.

It must all be a very interesting dream of being sick and in the new hospital that Dr. Amick built. The ka-lump-ka-lumping sound was a big part of the dream, and a smaller whishing sound was coming from an open slot like a mail drop. It called to Alice Ann to come and breathe in the nice, cool air it had inside. How magic was that? Air coming like from a fan in the wall of her little room Mother had called an "oxygen tent." Well, it was like a kind of tent over the top of half of her, and she closed her mouth around the opening to feel the new air go all the way down to her tummy ... a kind of foresty taste and smell, Alice Ann thought. She should make a poem about this dream so she wouldn't forget it, ever. But instead, there were her fingers digging across the itching on her cheeks and into her hair. And sure enough, there came Daddy again with the fingernail scissors.

Dreaming was always exciting. When she was a very small girl, Alice Ann had prayed to God for her to dream every single night, and sure enough it happened, something to make her respect God even more than before. The dream inside her oxygen tent that she liked best was about the bull fighting she could see outside her window: the red cape of the bull-fighter and the big black bull and the blood gushing all over the trees that grew right there in the bull-fighting ring.

Mother tried to tell her that it was just a picture on the wall across the room; she took the picture down and brought it over for Alice Ann to see up close, and sure enough, it was a painting of a round black bowl full of red flowers and green leaves. The minute Mother put it back, though, there was the bull moving toward the bull-fighter and the trees were waving every which way to get out of the way of all the blood.

After awhile Alice Ann could tell that she wasn't in the submarine like before. She was in a bed with the oxygen tent covering her top half and the ka-lumping sound came from a kind of pump putting nice fresh air into the tent. The person she'd thought was a Chinaman was really Nurse Beuschausen, Alice Ann's own private nurse. Her black hair was so pulled back from her face that it looked painted on and her eyes were kind of slanty. Once while the temperature-taker was in her mouth, Alice Ann looked up to see Nurse Beuschausen crying. She did look sad, and maybe Mother would know what was making her sad. She started to ask, but it was another one of the times when her head felt heavy and the words coming out of her mouth were strange and wavy. Part of the dream, she thought.

Another thing to wonder about was Mother or Daddy always sitting beside the bed. Alice Ann would smile at them, and then when she looked again, they were wearing different clothes than before. Once Mother's dress was the blue one, and when Alice Ann turned her head away and shut her eyes for just a minute, Mother had on the green dress with white dots. Same thing with Daddy; he would have his hat and coat on and whiskers from not shaving, and then the next minute she looked, he was shaved and wore a Sunday tie.

One day when the dreams went away and her words came out straight, Alice Ann wondered to Mother where was the blue dress she'd had on a minute ago, and Mother said, almost crossly, "Now-Ann-that-dress-was-on-me-days-ago."

The whole thing of being sick was very strange, the very strangest thing that she'd ever known, with always her throat and chest heavy and hot and nothing tasting good. Why did she have to be in the hospital where they didn't know how to make custard like

Mother? Once Alice Ann was out of the oxygen tent, she'd tell them to have Mother go to the hospital kitchen and make a batch of really good custard.

Dr. Amick came to see her almost as much as Daddy; she supposed it was because he wanted her to get well. Being so sick with double pneumonia wasn't so bad after Dr. Amick said the Crisis came, whatever that was, and her fever broke. It was then that she could sort out all the happenings and dreams to kind of put them in lists inside her head to pull out later and think about.

It was easy to imagine being a kind of Alice in Wonderland. She hadn't exactly followed the white rabbit down the rabbit hole, but there was a strangely different country with all kinds of adventures. Most of the time there was needing grown-ups to steer her through the swampy, scary places.

As soon as Dr. Amick and the nurse took away the oxygen tent, Alice Ann could finally think straight and not wonder if maybe she was imagining everything that happened.

"Alice Ann, now hold very still. You'll feel a little prick." It was Dr. Amick explaining that the needle would put to sleep the skin underneath her left arm, so that she'd never feel the hole made in her side and the long, fat rubber tube stuck into it, long enough to go almost to the floor below and into a big Mason jar that sat there and collected yellowish, greenish stuff coming from Alice Ann's insides. It was called "pus."

The whole story was that she had gobs of pus all over and around her lungs where she breathed. There was so much of the awful stuff that it squinched her lungs kind of flat, not letting them fill up with the air she breathed through her nose. That was why the oxygen tent had been such a good thing to use with kids like her who might have double pneumonia. She asked Daddy whatever happened to someone with double p. and who didn't have an oxygen tent to help them breathe. All of a sudden Daddy's eyes filled with tears. He squeezed her hand real tight and said they simply died.

Wow! Alice Ann felt really lucky to be in Dr. Amick's new hospital where he made her well and not dead. Wondering about that prayer she'd prayed lots of nights, Alice Ann began to think she must be extra careful about things to pray for.

She was definitely special these days; there was a ton of get-well cards from people she knew and some she didn't. There was a bouquet of fresh flowers from the Drama Club, a bunch of ladies who had Alice Ann act in a play they put on at the high school auditorium. Think of that! Real live flowers in the wintertime! Over on the window sill was the Valentine box from fourth grade, all filled up with valentines and Get-Well-Alice Ann cards. She couldn't believe that it was already February, almost the end of February. She'd been in that bed for a very long time.

Mother got tears in the corners of her eyes when she said that for quite awhile they didn't know if Alice Ann would ever get well from double pneumonia. It felt funny to hear about everybody in town praying for her not to die. Even Saint Josaphat's Church had a Mass for the photographer's daughter to get well. That made Alice Ann sorry all over again that she'd prayed for something to happen to make her feel important. All she'd meant for God to arrange for was a broken arm like Jo Ann's or maybe the mumps like Paul had and got to miss school for a week or two, not *two months* already! Maybe if all that pus didn't come out into the Mason jar, she'd even have to be in the hospital longer.

Each morning, bright and early, Nurse Beuschausen came in with an empty jar to take the place of the one under Alice Ann's bed. It was good to get rid of that stuff that caused double p., but how much more had to come out? Nobody seemed to know, not even Dr. Amick. One thing to be very thankful for was not using the oxygen tent anymore. Once while they thought she was sleeping, Daddy said to Mother how expensive each big can of oxygen was: twenty-five dollars. It was hard to remember how many times the man brought a new one in to stand there beside the bed, but that was while she was what Mother called: "not herself." The awfully high fever made her see things that weren't there. "One hundred and four degrees for two weeks, Alice Ann," Dr. Amick told her while he patted her shoulder and smiled kind of sad. "But you're a tough little ten-year-old, I'll say that for you." He did a strange thing for a doctor then; he leaned over the kissed her cheek.

Ladies from the American Legion Auxiliary came to see her when she still didn't feel like talking. There were sores inside her mouth from the fever. One lady, Mrs. Olson, brought her boy with her. Alice Ann felt sorry for him while he stood close to the door, twisting his cap in his hands and staring at the ceiling. Bob was in sixth grade, she remembered, but his mother kept calling him "Bobby." Mrs. Olson said, "Alice Ann, we of the auxiliary know how much you like to read, and we want to order a special book for you as a get-well gift. Is there one that you especially would like better than any other?"

It was hard to know why she said what she did then, but it was all kind of tied up with watching Bob. It was plain that he hadn't even wanted to come. Before she knew it, she was saying nice and loud so maybe he'd hear: "Treasure Island by Robert Louis Stevenson." When they'd gone, Alice Ann tried to think why she hadn't said "Anne of Green Gables" or "Little Women." Her head ached with wondering, but Dr. Amick came in just then to put her side to sleep for another hole to suck out the pus and make her well. Having double p. wasn't the best thing that ever happened to her.

With God-blesses at night, Alice Ann prayed to get well soon, if that was okay. Lying in bed all day was bad when outside it was starting spring. The way she could tell was from the dresser mirror across her room. In it everything was always backwards, making things reflected look like a different town with the street and stores and sidewalks all turned around.

Her bed couldn't be moved closer, so Nurse Beuschausen pulled the dresser close to the window where you could see the first morning light reflected on store windows and Mr. Vodendahl unlocking his hardware store, opening the door to start sweeping the walk. He did it every morning the same, first banging a big broom against the iron railing to shake last night's inside dust loose, she guessed. Then, back and forth he'd go, with long sweeps to stop when Miss Ann Van came by on her way to work. Mr. Vodendahl would lean the broom against his shoulder and take off his cap, smile and say something Alice Ann couldn't hear, only imagine, like: "Good mornin', Miss Van. A fine mornin', isn't it?" Miss Ann Van would nod, but keep walking on her very high heels.

It was a special thing to look forward to every day, like the breakfast tray and the "spit bath" Nurse Beuschausen gave. There was a big basin of warm water and a fluffy wash cloth covered with soap to reach every part of Alice Ann, except the holes in her side. You couldn't see them, but you could feel them, all covered with yellow medicine Dr. Amick put there. It would keep away infection, he said.

At first there was just one hole to suck the pus out; then there was another, the one that made Dr. Amick cuss while he was cutting it. It was kind of a worry to hear him say kind of soft, but angry: "God-damn-it-to-hell!" the way Daddy cussed when the pipes in the darkroom froze that time. Alice Ann looked quick at the nurse helping, to see if she was surprised to hear Dr. Amick taking the Lord's name in vain.

That night she prayed hard for God to forgive Dr. Amick's breaking the commandment. She prayed it twice since it sure wouldn't do for him to go to Hell when he died. Alice Ann had done the same thing after she walked into the darkroom to hear Daddy cussing a blue streak at the frozen water pipes flooding the floor all over. She hurried out before he saw her and crawled under the dining room table. First she cried and then she prayed for God to forgive Daddy and to understand that he wasn't a big swearer like Harv O'Brian, who'd never make it to Heaven with all his cussing. It had taken her quite awhile to figure out when Harv said "Suns-up britches," he wasn't talking about early morning trousers.

Taking all the pus out was connected with getting well. It didn't seem to be happening fast enough, even though the fever dreams were gone. Now though, Alice

Ann's hair started coming out in big clumps. Dr. Amick said the high fever for a long time did it. Surely now, it was time to be all well and go home. Jane Ellen was walking all over the place, Mother said, but she couldn't come to the hospital. It was just one more reason for getting well quick.

With all her heart, Alice Ann wanted to speed up the Recovery. That was the word Nurse Pichota used for getting well. There were all sorts of new words to remember, like Cri-sis and Sur-ger-y and In-cu-ba-tion and Hy-po and Vis-i-tat-tion and Ter-mi-nal. A lady in the next room was that word: terminal. Finding out what it meant made Alice Ann sad. The lady would not get well and would die soon. Listening at night when everything was quiet, she heard the nurses talking down at the nurses' station; it made her smile to think of a train chug-chugging down the hall when someone said the word "station."

Sounds and smells were a big part of each night and day. The soft swish of Nurse Pichota's white skirt and the squeak of her shoes told Alice Ann of her coming down the hall, even from far away. And the minute they took the oxygen tent away, smells from the kitchen downstairs came creeping up to tell what she'd have on lunch tray. One of the best smells was Dr. Amick's shaving lotion when he walked in. The sound of his voice was kind of smiley, with a little chuckle some-times. It was fun to hear him teasing the nurses and coming closer and closer to her room. She closed her eyes then and prayed that he was coming to see her. When he went on by, Alice Ann kept her eyes shut and imagined him walk-walk-walking, step by step, swing-ing one arm and holding things called "files" up close to his doctor coat with the other. Inside her head, she made a picture of Dr. Amick stopping, turning around and coming back to her room. It was easy to imagine him smiling and shaking his head, kind of like remembering that he needed to see how the photographer's daughter was doing. There in her mind, it was simple to turn him around and bring him back to her door. And hey! Sometimes it worked!

One day Alice Ann forgot to think about it and Dr. Amick surprised her, walking in with another doctor named Dr. Weinberg. He was from Omaha and looked very important with glasses down on his nose and a stethoscope like Dr. Amick's hanging around his neck. Dr. Weinberg checked her all over, even the holes taking out the pus. Then he sat down, cleared his throat and asked, "Alice Ann, are you tired of being sick? Well, I have invented an operation to make you well. There's a boy in Omaha about your age who was every bit as sick as you, and today he's running around and playing ball because of the operation I performed on him. How about it? I can operate on you and at the same time teach Dr. Amick my tricks. But you must make the decision for me to do it."

She'd heard the word before: decision. But it was hard to remember what it meant. Maybe it was a cousin of "incision," but she didn't want to ask and seem dumb. Dr. Amick smiled his big smile that said everything would be okay. So Alice Ann smiled, too, and nodded yes and decided she loved him right then and there.

Nurse Beuschausen had strong arms. She could lift you with just one movement when she changed the bedsheets. On the day for Alice Ann to sit in a chair for the first time, it seemed like Daddy should help lift, but he stood aside for Nurse Beuschausen to sweep her strong arms around and under, and before you could say "Jack Robinson," there Alice Ann was, sitting in the chair close to the window, looking out at things right side around and not backwards like in the mirror.

For the first time in lots and lots of weeks, she was at least out of the hospital bed, trying to think how many days she'd spent there, but her brain got tired from the adding up. It was funny to sit there, like a Raggedy Ann doll with floppy arms and floppier legs.

"Now-Alice-Ann-sit-real-still-for-Dora-to-give-you-a-nice-haircut," Mother said in a fast, whispery voice. She held the paper sack for the pieces of cut-off hair and paid Dora fifty cents when the cutting was finished. It took a long time, maybe since there were hard scabs mixed up in the hair. Alice Ann had scratched her head, making it bleed while she was in the oxygen tent, but most all of it was healed up. She wasn't sure just why she'd done that. Sometimes it had been when nobody came in the room for a long time, and other times it happened when she worried about how Daddy could ever pay for all that time it took to get her well. Pulling the scabs off had hurt, but somehow the hurting felt right, like maybe a reminder to be awfully careful about what she prayed for, especially wanting to feel special.

Dora told her, "Alice Ann, your hair might still come out in big clumps. I've seen it before, when people had a very high fever for a long time. Your hair is bound to come back in, and right now I've shaped it while I cut, making do. After your operation, I'll come back to do some more."

Oh, yes, the operation. Alice Ann had almost forgotten it. But that same day, here came Dr. Weinberg from Omaha and Dr. Amick, too, walking in, smiling like she was really something special. Nurse Beuschausen lifted her onto a skinny table with wheels, then moved it fast out into the hall and down to the operating room.

"All right, Alice Ann, we're going to make you good as new," Dr. Weinberg said, patting her shoulder and nodding to somebody who turned on a bright light and put a kind of cup over her nose. Then, "How would you like to go on a rocket ship to the moon?" She started to answer: "Just like Buck Rogers?" but before she could finish saying it, she was right there in a rocket ship being whizzed so fast it was hard to breathe. There were stars zooming alongside her in the brightest colors she'd ever seen. They sparkled and fizzed like strange firecrackers, but one thing was different. They didn't make a sound, not even a little whoosh. Everything around her was quiet, no sound anywhere.

When she was about high enough, she thought she might just see Heaven, someone from faraway asked, "Alice Ann … Alice Ann … can you hear me?" It was Dr. Amick right up close to her face, but his voice came from across the room. Tiredness made her want to keep quiet and sleep, but the voice kept calling her name from faraway. Opening her eyes, Alice Ann saw that she was in a different room with strange ceiling and walls, and someone had filled her mouth with cotton. She tried spitting it out, but no luck; and then Mother was holding her hand real tight.

"Alice Ann, you've had your operation. Now you must wake up." It was Dr. Amick, holding her other hand and talking right from his mouth, not across the room.

"You have a long incision in your side. Dr. Weinberg put a rubber apron inside your chest between your ribs to collect all the rest of the poison pus that wouldn't let you get well." He said more words, but they started coming from somewhere else again. She wanted to go back to the rocket ship, but people in the room kept talking and laughing and making her stay awake.

Dr. Amick came close again and said ever so softly and kindly, "You do need to stay awake, Alice Ann. There is a big bandage around you now, but soon we'll take it off and remove the rubber apron."

It was pretty clear that certain words you knew could mean something different to other people. Knowing that was part of growing up, she guessed. Take the word: "apron." It meant only one thing to Alice Ann; in her mind she could see Mother's kitchen apron hanging on the hook behind the back door, sometimes fresh and clean and other times spotted with bacon grease that spattered and brown gravy that dribbled. An apron was always an apron, even the little half-one that Mother wore when Ladies' Auxiliary met at the studio. It was pale green and ruffly with a flower embroidered on the pocket. And it never got dirty.

Why then, did Dr. Weinberg from Omaha call the poison-pus collector inside Alice Ann an apron? She couldn't see it and couldn't feel it, even if it was made of sponge rubber like Dr. Amick explained. He told her that "apron" was a medical term, for doctors to understand. The best thing to do was to nod just like you understood and then wonder about it at night when all the hospital was quiet and you couldn't sleep yet. There were quite a lot of those wonderings.

The day they took the apron out, Daddy stood beside her bed and held her hand real tight. First the bandages came off and with them the most awful smell Alice Ann would ever smell. What was scary was that the terrible smell came from her, and maybe to keep her mind off what was coming next, she said out loud: "I smell like a dead goat!" Now why did that pop out? She'd never seen or smelled a dead goat. But it made Daddy laugh and even Dr. Amick did. She guessed that she'd made a good joke.

For sure it was the only thing to laugh about that day. Next thing that happened was the apron being pulled out from where it had been maybe two or three days. She wasn't sure. What was for sure was the breath-taking-away BIG pain that came in her chest like a red-hot poker from a stove.

She'd been getting ready to feel the little needle prick like before when Dr. Amick put her side to sleep for making the holes there. This time there wasn't any prick, just the most awful, AWFUL hurting she could remember ever having. Another bad thing was Daddy letting loose of her hand to go outside the room. All she could do then was grab hold of the iron side of the bed and yell out bloody murder!

It seemed like the pain would never stop, but in a little while it was all over. Nurse Pichota wiped away Alice Ann's tears. Mother came to say that Daddy had felt real sick all of a sudden standing there by her bed. That's why he left so fast. Well, a hospital is the very best place to be if you feel sick, she guessed.

Dr. Amick showed Nurse Pichota how to do some-thing called "irrigating" inside the incision: a squirt-ing in of disinfectant, he said. To be sure there wasn't any poison pus, she decided. The hurting was still there, so then there was a pill to help it go away and some salve for her lip where she'd bitten it clean through. Everything got taken care of that day. And she'd be out of the hospital soon. But before she went to sleep, Alice Ann promised God with all her heart that she'd be satisfied not to feel special for a long, long time.

* * * * *

Getting well was the only thing to work at, Dr. Amick told her each day. It was always early in the morning, sometimes before breakfast tray, that he came to see her. He walked in all smiley and sat on the bed beside her like Alice Ann was the only one he cared about seeing that day. Then he watched Nurse Pichota do the irrigating thing in the long hole, nodding and grinning from ear to ear with a kind of proudness.

She was too shy to tell him that she loved him. And it was hard to tell him thank you for bringing Dr. Weinberg from Omaha, like Mother said she should. Once, when he was listening to her chest with his stethoscope, she almost came out with the thank-you thing. Instead, she got tears in her eyes and a lump where she swallowed. Maybe Dr. Amick could tell how she felt, because he took both her hands in his and whispered, "Alice Ann, after all we've been through together, I think of myself as your other daddy. Is that okay with you?"

It was a secret for just the two of them, she guessed. She wrote down those words he said in her Christmas diary and locked it with the little key she kept in the bedside table drawer. It might hurt Ellen's feelings if she bragged about what Dr. Amick had said. The very knowing it was something not to forget for a million years. It made a warm blanket feeling over her every

92

time Alice Ann thought of it.

This hospital room had a window facing into back-yards of houses. Mostly there were trees lining back fences, but the one where Coach Brown lived didn't have trees blocking the yard and back porch where the clothesline started and hooked up to a pole that leaned.

It helped the days go by to watch that far backyard, even if nobody came out the back porch door. It seemed like Mrs.. Brown never hung her washing on the line. It was easy to make up a poem in her head about the washrag hung at the end of the line, waiting to be used to clean the wire, but never getting to. It was a dingy little scrap of cloth. One day a robin sat on it, pecked at it, and flew away with threads from it in his beak, maybe to use in a nest.

Mother said for sure she didn't believe that Alice Ann saw that far down the block, and maybe she dreamed it. Dreaming was something to know apart from the real thing. There had been enough dreams to last her forever. There were times that grown-ups didn't believe you; then you should just keep from telling, but for sure write it down the way it happened.

One other thing she wrote about in her diary was the rubber ball they had her blow up three times a day. Dr. Amick said it was the inside part to a football that kept the air to make the ball round and hard. When he brought it in the first time, he said, "See how flat it is now? That's how your lungs were once, squeezed flat. They're not anymore, but they need to get some exercise and be full of air again. Blowing up this ball, Alice Ann, will help your lungs recover."

She would do anything for Dr. Amick. She'd jump

off the Loup River Bridge if he asked her to. The blowing into the ball was hard at first, but it got easier every time she did it. Dr. Amick told Daddy that Alice Ann should play a wind instrument in the school band. That was exciting, especially to think of sitting by Gene Olcott, the sixth-grader who swung his trombone case around in last-bell line and almost hit her. He was one of the bad boys from across town, but Alice Ann thought he looked like a tough-guy movie star.

Something to worry Daddy and Mother was when Dr. Amick listening to her chest, sat back and shook his head, doctor-like. He told them that Alice Ann had a "heart murmur," whatever that was. She did sometimes have a feeling in her chest like a little fish flopping over, but not all the time. Only once in awhile. If she started blowing into a trombone, that flopping murmur might go away. And in grade school band, maybe she'd get to sit beside Gene Olcott. Wow!

It was a whole lot of something to look forward to, even if the exact day for her to go home hadn't been decided. Lying in bed, watching the trees by the window beginning to have little leaves, listening to the soft patter of spring rain made her start to think up poems inside her head. They were all about how it would feel to finally go home to the studio and Ned and Baby Jane and Daddy and Mother.

> *I like to live in this world today,*
> *I'm glad that I can work and play .*
> *I'm glad that I can breathe and see.*
> *It seems like this world was made for me.*
> *I feel that I could dance and sing,*
> *This world is so full of everything.*

It had been winter when she got carried into Dr.

Amick's new hospital. Now it was spring when they'd come to take her home so she could finish up getting over double p. Alice Ann listened carefully to the talking just outside her room and heard that two nurses would carry her down the steps. Daddy would be waiting with a rented car.

It was okay that she couldn't walk very well yet. Being so sick for so long had made her legs forget how to move across the floor even two steps. Once she was home and could practice, walking was sure to happen, and then running would be next, like Dr. Weinberg from Omaha had promised.

Needing to stay in the hospital for a long time had made a lot of thinking to go on in Alice Ann's head. Wondering about things could make you smarter. She wanted so much to understand all the things grown-ups knew, and not have to keep asking questions, or worse, stay quiet and keep wondering.

When would knowing happen? In two more years, maybe? Or three? It was hard to stay a kid for so long and be treated like a little kid. Yes, she was sure that being in that hospital bed for almost four months with nothing to do but rest and have spit baths and irrigations and turn wonderings around inside her head, for sure had made her smarter. Maybe smarter than most fifth-graders.

"Alice Ann, you'll-maybe-need-to-take-fifth-grade-over-since-you've-missed-so-much-school-now-think-about-it." What an awful thing to think about! Well, sixth grade arithmetic would be kind of hard to work without the last half of fifth grade, which she'd missed. Maybe if she worked on it all summer? It wouldn't be much fun to spend the summer on arithmetic. Her head ached with thinking and worrying about it.

Being grown-up with no worries would be sooo good. Being adult was the word for it. Just saying "adult" sounded so tall and smart and knowing about everything. Somehow, though, it was mysterious and maybe a little bit forbidden. After all, didn't the Seventh Commandment say: "Thou shalt not commit adultery?" In Sunday School while you memorized the rules that Moses brought down the mountain, you never got to really talk about them and ask questions. Only grownups knew all the meanings of all the words.

Reverend Petersen's girl Shirley told Alice Ann what she knew about adultery and how they shouldn't talk about it. Okay, she promised never to tell Mother or Daddy about the kind of funny pictures Shirley drew on her tablet of a lady and man doing "adultery." Before Alice Ann had a good long look at them, Shirley tore them up. Well, she'd grown up a little bit in the hospital, but not far enough to be adult, not yet anyway.

When the day came for going home, it was a strange sensation. That was her latest new word: "sensation." Dr. Amick said it when she first stood up out of bed: "Alice Ann, do you feel any sensation in your legs?" She had to ask him what it meant, kind of knowing but not for sure. Then finding out it was another word for "feeling," she decided to use it all the time.

She asked Daddy, "What is your sensation about having me home again after so long?" It made him laugh; then he told her it was a good sensation, the sooner the quicker. That was a kind of joke between them. Instead of saying "the sooner, the better" like it should be, once Ned said "the sooner the quicker" when he was trying to act smart. Then she and Daddy never said it the right way.

It would be wonderful to be a family again and have jokes happen like before. But when the day came to be glad, Alice Ann needed to sort out being happy from being sorry to leave Nurse Beuschausen and Nurse Pichota. They were almost like her family. Mother had told her that when Nurse Pichota thought the photographer's daughter was dying, she went up to the nurses' room on third floor and cried for a long time. Nurses were special, for sure. Maybe it would be just as good as being a photographer, to be a nurse. The "sensation" of helping people get well would be swell.

What took up a whole lot of the morning that day was practicing how to say good-bye to Dr. Amick. After all, he'd said that he felt like her second daddy, so maybe he'd be sad to see her leave the hospital. But no, he wouldn't be sad. He'd be glad. She wanted to say thank you for getting Dr. Weinberg from Omaha to do the incision. But how to say it without sounding like a real little kid was bothersome. Should she just shake his hand or maybe hug his neck? It mustn't be like play-acting, whatever she did. Inside her head, Alice Ann played it out, one way first, then another way, all the time wanting him to know how extra special he was. Just once she wanted to come close to his doctor coat and smell the clean, medicine smell. One more time she wanted him to lean over and kiss the top of her head, and smile his nice "you're special" smile.

Maybe it would be best just to wait and say something like a grown-up would tell him, like: "It's been real nice to know you." But all of a sudden the nurses were there with her coat and tam, and Mother with a grocery sack to carry home things from the bedside table. Nurse Beuschausen and Nurse Pichota made a kind of seat with their hands for Alice Ann to sit in going down the stairs to the front door and then to the rented car. Everybody seemed to be in a terrible hurry to get her out of the hospital, and Dr. Amick wasn't even there yet. She sure didn't want to leave the hospital right that minute, so she asked where Dr. Amick was.

"Alice Ann, Dr. Amick is in surgery now. He's performing the same operation on someone as he did on you. And he's right in the middle of it." Nurse Pichota said that and reached into her nurse's uniform pocket for a handkerchief to wipe away the tears that kept coming and coming down Alice Ann's cheeks. She just couldn't stop them even inside the car.

HOMECOMING CAN HAPPEN

"Alice Ann-better-stop-those-tears-and-start-smiling-again." Mother's voice was happy and tight-sounding at the same time, but her hand reaching from the back seat was gentle on Alice Ann's shoulder. She knew it was a reminder to know it was time for her to start thinking about living in the studio again where customers might be watching and listening to find out how the photographer's daughter was doing out of the hospital. Mother didn't say it, but the sound of her voice was enough.

It was kind of easy to begin smiling, especially when Daddy took the long way home, around the two blocks west of the hospital, and then turned down the full length of Main Street. All that Alice Ann saw seemed brighter and bigger than she remembered. Mayor Gdanitz must've repainted the front of his 5 and 10. Swanson's Drug Store sign shouted at her, almost like it was already turned on in the daytime. Trees around the courthouse were lots taller and greener than before; even the corner fire plug shone brighter and redder. Every store window was sparkling like being freshly washed, and the post office flag fluttered without any ragged edges.

It was all something to marvel at, but not out loud, for fear she was the only one seeing things like brand new. Writing about it in her Christmas diary, she promised to tell everything exactly the way it seemed — fresh and clean and standing out different from the way she remembered.

Surely she wasn't the first kid to have that "sensation." That new word was a good one for describing the going-home day, the town and the people; it meant something bigger than just a "feeling" on the day she felt new, too.

When Daddy pulled up in the alley beside the studio's front door, there was Ned hopping up and down. His hair was combed for once, and his smile showed two more teeth missing. Alice Ann opened the car door before Daddy could get out and around, then swung her legs out and stood leaning there.

"Are you all well? How d'y'feel, Alice Ann?" Ned's voice was older-sounding. She wished she had the right words to tell him how good she felt. Then she remembered and almost before she thought about it, the feeling became a word.

Alice Ann heard herself yelling back to Ned, "Hey, I feel *sensation-full!*" It was a good thing that Daddy caught her when she tried to run with what Nurse Pichota had called her "rubber legs," and everybody laughed.

Helen and Doc were there with Jane Ellen. Helen put her arms around Alice Ann and said, "I think you mean 'sensation-al,' sweetheart." It wouldn't be any use to try explaining that the other word was better sounding. Maybe there wasn't such a word as "sensation-full." She knew there really should be. It was better at describing how she felt that day: alive and new and special and God-blessed.

When she pulled off her hat inside the studio and looked into the mirror there, Alice Ann could see new red hair coming in where the old had come out, and wonder of wonders! It sure looked curly! Mother stood behind her and agreed that there were real live curls in place of the old straight hair. For a minute while they were both there in the mirror, Alice Ann had the strangest sensation that they both smiled the same way, with the same surprised and happy look. But no, it couldn't be. Mother was old, like maybe 37 or even older. Her eyes were bright blue, where Alice Ann's were blue-green with yellow dots like Aunt Fan's, hair was auburn like Mammy Potter's, and a dimple in her chin just like Daddy's.

Mother held under Alice Ann's arms to guide her to the bedroom, and the bed looked so good. She was tireder than she remembered being for a long time. All through the undressing and into brand new p.j.s, the picture of them together in the mirror kept coming back, and along with it the same new sensation as with the 5 and 10 and the drug store sign and the fire plug and the flag.

The whole thing was something to write down and never to forget. She would write that it was like being on the edge of something that you couldn't see, but knew was there waiting. It was what she'd call a different place on top of the old place before she got double p. Not scary, but exciting to think about and wonder at and maybe even see in dreams. The truly hard part of it was knowing that she could never ever go back.

Coming home meant a whole new set of smells. She'd been in the hospital for so long that its smells were maybe locked into her nose. Breathing in the new smells of the studio was almost like arriving in a different country where the sweeping compound smell and the developer and the photographic paper smells were something 'way back in memory, wrapping around her now and tickling her nose until she sneezed at the strangeness.

"We'd-best-get--you-into-bed-Alice Ann," Mother was saying in her take-charge voice, and soon the next smell was Fels-Naptha from her pillowcase. It was only the laundry soap that Mother used all the time, but it was still too exciting to even think about going to sleep. Her body was tired, but not her mind or her eyes. There was Jane Ellen trotting all over the place, wanting to get into bed with Alice Ann and then wanting down the minute she was in. Helen and Doc stayed long enough to give her a big box of chocolates from Farnhams' Drugstore. It was special to have rich friends like them, who sometimes loaned Daddy their car and stayed with Ned and Jane Ellen and brought supper more times than Mother could remember.

"Alice Ann-we-will-move-you-into-your-very-own-room-soon-as-I-get-the-curtains-up." Mother let her know that Daddy had had Harv O'Brien cut windows in the studio south wall where she could look out on Uncle Ashley's driveway. Not just one window, but two brand-new ones that went up and down slicker than any of the others in the studio. Ned showed her how a dozen times. And there were two new walls closing in that corner of the Heavy Room to make Alice Ann's private room. The walls weren't all the way to the ceiling since it was so high, and Daddy could see above them when he was coming down from the frame room. The door opening out into the photo-taking part had only a creton curtain hanging there; customers might peek in to see Alice Ann lying there in bed. Until the hole in her side was all healed up by itself, with no stitches, Alice Ann needed to stay in bed, not walking very much yet.

Nurse Pichota came every day with what Ned called a long squirt gun filled with special water to rinse out Alice Ann's hole where the rubber apron had been. Dr. Weinberg said the incision would heal up in no time, and then there wouldn't be any need for the "irrigating." Alice Ann giggled every time she thought of that word in connection with her. All she'd ever seen irrigated was a garden.

Visitors were the best thing that happened while she waited to be healed. She kept track of all the ones who came to see her and a list of the presents that they brought. The Methodist Church Ladies' Aid came with a big wicker basket holding little wrapped packages, one to open each day of a whole week. First was a nice comb in its own crocheted holder. Alice Ann tried it and filled it up with hair that was still coming out. When she remembered praying to God for curly hair, she wondered if being sick all that long time was worth having brand new hair. Ellen made a joke about her short hair looking like a boy's, but before she left the studio she said ever so softly, "Maybe I'll get my hair cut short like yours, Alice Ann." It was a friendly thing to do.

Lying there being quiet for so long in the hospital had made Alice Ann watch and listen to people more than before. It was fun to watch their faces and try to figure out what they were really thinking. Clara in Cleaning at the hospital had been one person good to watch and listen to. She talked to Alice Ann like they were the same age, scrubbing the floor and wiping windows and telling all of the things that went on inside the hospital and downtown, even at her own house where her mom and pap talked only Polish. Even when Clara talked a blue streak, it was easy to see when she was sad inside.

Face-watching was a bit harder with Nurse Pichota and Dr. Amick. Sometimes with pretend-closed eyes, she'd listen and watch when they thought she was asleep. It was a game to play without them knowing; maybe if she practiced enough, she'd get real good at reading other people's thinking.

When Uncle Ashley and Aunt Belle came to see her, Alice Ann watched them while they talked about the weather and the cafe where Uncle Ashley helped out, but she could almost tell what they were thinking: "That poor little girl lying there with a hole in her side and hair coming out and maybe never getting well." It was there in their eyes, kind of sad with their mouths saying things to cheer her up. Well, she'd show them! She *was* going to get well and run and play like the boy in Omaha. She knew it, but didn't tell them, just smiled. It would be her very own secret surprise to hold onto until she was back skating up and down on the sidewalk in front of Aunt Belle's house.

When she was finally on what Mother called "the-road-to-recovery," Alice Ann discovered that every day wasn't sensation-full like at the beginning. The best days were when visitors came. Those days, she made a star on the page in the Christmas diary; if it was a real special visitor, she put a circle all around the star. Days that Dr. Amick came, she drew three stars after he'd gone out the door. The first time he stayed a long time, inspecting her incision and smiling his I-like-you smile, holding her hand and touching the new curly hair ever so softly.

Another three-star day was the one when her trombone arrived. Daddy brought it from Elsners' Jewelry Store. "This is just what the doctor ordered," he said with a wink and laughing at the joke he'd made. Alice Ann couldn't wait to open the leather case and take out the pieces that when they were put together would make her trombone. She wasn't sure how to do it.

"Alice Ann-you-wait-until-the-music-teacher-comes-to-show-you," Mother said. She left the open case sitting there for Alice Ann to run her hands over the shininess, around and inside and under the big bell. (That's what Doc told her it was when he came to see.) Doc played an instrument in City Band, but it wasn't the trombone, so he couldn't explain things.

Kids had it hard, waiting for things to happen. Grown-ups just didn't understand how long the time could be between knowing something was coming and the real thing happening. She knew that Mr. Sell was a busy teacher, so she didn't keep asking "when-when-when" the way Ned always did.

Thank goodness the day for Alice Ann's first lesson came when there weren't customers being photographed. Dr. Amick had said she could sit in a chair for one hour at a time, three times a day. So there she was, like magic all of a sudden, with Mr. Sell "demonstrating." A new word for the new day, so then she used it whenever she could.

With the first lesson barely over, she told Ned that she would demonstrate how to put the pieces of the trombone together properly, where to oil the slide and empty the spit valve. She tried to do it like Mr. Sell had demonstrated, but all Ned wanted to do was blow into the mouthpiece with no sound coming out. Alice Ann had to tell him to make a kind of prissy smile and put the mouthpiece up to it, then act like he was spitting a hair off his tongue. That would make a good trombone sound. Wrinkling up his face and trying so hard made Alice Ann laugh, but after about the fourth or fifth time he actually made a kind of "toot." She told him it was almost as good as she did.

It was a beautiful trombone with the name "Beuscher" cut right into the metal in fancy whirly-type letters. She decided that must be the name of the man who made it. Right then and there, she named her trombone the whirly-lettered name: "Beuscher." When you said it, it sounded important and kind of mysterious. Daddy said it wasn't a brand new instrument. It was used. Someone before her had held Beuscher and played in a band maybe, and marched in a parade, maybe. Whoever it was, they'd taken good care of Beuscher; there were only a few little scratches on the outside slide if you looked real hard. She rubbed them and polished to get them out, but no luck.

Mr. Sell told her that Beuscher had good tone; that meant the sound that came out when he played it. Alice Ann would need to practice a very long time before she'd get the awfully good tone that Mr. Sell could make without even puffing. He so easily smiled into the mouthpiece, blew his cheeks out a bit, and then brought the silvery sound to make her shiver, thinking someday she might be able to do the same lovely sound.

Fifth grade had been when you could sign up for

instrument lessons, but Alice Ann had known there wasn't money enough to even rent one, so she hadn't asked back in September. She was already taking piano lessons from Jo Ann's mother, and they were paid for by Mother sewing for the Thompsons, dresses for Jo Ann and her sisters. Once there was enough material left over to make Alice Ann a dress like Jo Ann's. It was blue and red and yellow plaid, and they saw to it that they wore their dresses to school sometimes on the very same day.

The remembering of how she'd prayed for something to happen to make her feel special kept coming to her mind. When she had double p., being prayed for by people she didn't know, and now looking like she was getting the curly Shirley-Temple hair she'd wanted, all that happening was too much to forget. Now, with Beuscher thrown in, too, something she had not prayed for, it was almost too much to understand.

Nights when the studio was all shut down and quiet, with everybody asleep but Alice Ann, she lay there in bed and kind of talked to God about how good everything was. She never did get any God-talk back, but still had the strangest feeling, like she was wrapped up in a great big smile. Her life seemed like a giant smile. Maybe that's what God wanted her to know, that things would be good from now on. She wrote more words to the "I Like to Live" poem:

The soft pink clouds, the golden grain,
The ribboned rainbow after rain,
The blazing sunset at close of day,
And fragrant scent of new-mown hay.
I feel like I could dance and sing,
This world is so full of everything!

I wish I had something to give
To show the world I like to live.

She added the words in her diary, so she wouldn't forget them. They just seemed to roll out of her head and onto the paper, faster than she could think them out loud. Maybe she'd be a poet like Mammy in Geneva when she grew up. She'd write a big book filled up with poems and sell it and pay Daddy for all the hospital bills that piled up while she was so very sick. Yes, that's just what she'd do!

The next day after was for sure a three-star day, maybe even special enough for four stars at the top of the diary page. It was so exciting when Nurse Beuschausen inspected the incision. She smiled a big smile and told Mother and Daddy that the hole was all healed up, with no more needing to be irrigated. Alice Ann let out a huge "Whoopee" before she remembered that there might be a customer coming in the door of the studio.

The next important thing was Dr. Amick coming by to inspect her side and say that Dr. Weinberg wanted Daddy to take photographs of the incision for a medical journal, whatever that was. She decided it must be like the books Daddy got from special photography people who published stories and pictures that were important for professionals to see. She liked the sound of that word: professional. It meant "important" for sure, but it was hard for her to work it into most conversations.

Thinking about having her picture in a book with stuff about Dr. Weinberg's operation that he invented and used on her was fun. Then Dr. Amick stayed for the picture-taking, showing her how to pose with her left arm up in the air, away from the side where the long closed-up hole was. It was a bit chilly, sitting there with no clothes on above her waist, but that was how the photo had to be taken.

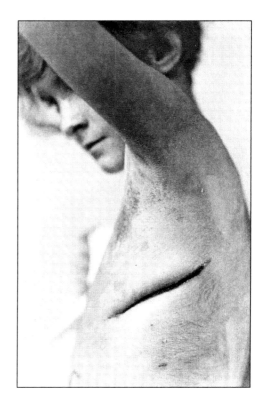

Alice Ann was used to having her picture taken. She knew how to hold real still, sometimes not even breathing. She was sure she'd been photographed two hundred times. The velvet baby book was full of her pictures, starting when she was even too little to sit up. Looking through the book, she imagined Daddy there behind the black cloth, focusing on her in the small enamel bathtub, the wicker baby buggy and the wooden pushcart, sitting at the little "heavy table," beside the Christmas tree, and on the long, soft bench with fringe. Then there she was with each Grandma, with Mother and Ned, but never with Daddy.

One day when Alice Ann was three, Daddy posed her to look like a famous painting that he liked. The painting was called "Age of Innocence," she found out later. All that was in her memory was sitting still for so long that it made her legs go to sleep. When the photo-taking was done and she could get down from the bench, those legs didn't work right and she fell down. *That* she remembered!

Daddy called the photograph "Smiling Innocence" because in it, Alice Ann was smiling. He made big enlargements of her sitting there in floaty kind of cloth Mother called "gauze," wrapped all around her. Mammy in Geneva wrote a poem about the picture, and it went like this:

> *I do not comb my hair this way,*
> *nor wear this kind of clothes.*
> *I'm just a picture for today;*
> *My daddy had me pose.*
> *A picture of another child,*
> *Long years before I grew.*
> *She lived and loved*
> *And wept and smiled*
> *The same as I shall do.*
>
> —*Lora Goodrich Potter*

Each of the grandparents was given one of the enlargements that Mother tinted with colored oils. Also, Helen and Doc got one, since they were Best Friends, Mother said. Her photograph was framed and put into the studio's big front window to show people who came by and might then want to have photos taken at Conger's Studio.

While Alice Ann sat there with her arm up for the incision pictures, she thought of all those other times posing in front of the giant painted background covering the whole east wall of the Heavy Room. No one called it that anymore, but she still thought of it like long ago.

There must have been five hundred pictures taken against that background: family groups and weddings and mothers with babies and high school graduations and first communions, all in front of that beautiful scene some artist had painted on the biggest piece of canvas you could imagine.

The painting looked like the inside of a magic castle, with tall windows and lovely curtains and huge vases holding flowers and a ledge that looked out on a garden. In her mind sometimes, Alice Ann walked right into the painted-on room and opened the painted-on window and leaned out on the painted-on ledge. Down below she could imagine a prince standing like in Cinderella, and she would blow him kisses like beautiful ladies did in the picture show at the Liberty.

When she saw it, the photo of Dr. Weinberg's incision in her side looked kind of ugly. It showed where the tape had left dirty-looking marks on her side where the bandages came off each time her hole got irrigated. Now that it was over, it all seemed like a long, bad dream.

It seemed ages ago that she first prayed to be special. And maybe God didn't answer that kind of prayer in exactly the way you wanted. She'd done lots of thinking about it while she was getting well. If God was love, like Jesus said, then almost dying was maybe not part of the Plan. Things just happened sometimes, like germs floating around and car drivers who weren't careful and lightning that started fires and airplanes that did crash. Maybe when she was twelve or thirteen, Alice Ann could understand more about life.

Now it was enough to walk in the sunshine halfway up the sidewalk beside Uncle Ashley's driveway;

the first time was the very best ... sensationful, like coming home from the hospital. It was warm enough to go bare-headed, but her old hair was still kind of scraggly and the new, short and fuzzy. She didn't stay outside very long because someone was always walking by and staring at her. She was very, very tired of being special.

The coming of summer was to be happy about, especially when it turned out that Alice Ann wouldn't need to study fifth grade arithmetic and English so she could pass on into sixth. She was secretly happy that it was something the grown-ups had to decide, that it would be best to stay back a year in school.

"You-were-always-the-youngest-in-your-class-since-starting-kindergarten-middle-of-November," Mother told her in a voice that sounded like it was a secret between them. "Now-you'll-be-where-you-should-have-been." And that was that. Alice Ann could tell by the tone of Mother's voice that it was no use asking or worse, arguing. There could come a look from Mother that made you feel an inch tall if you argued about something that was already decided.

Maybe it was to make up for feeling sorry a bit about taking fifth grade over that Daddy and Mother told Ned and Alice Ann the news that they could take summer Reading Lessons from Mrs. Ada Mason. She lived in the richest part of town and knew all there was to know about memorizing poetry and something called prose, and how to pronounce all words the right way.

Ned said it didn't sound like fun; he wanted to spend all summer playing ball and fishing. He heard that Mrs. Ada Mason had recitals like a piano teacher and her pupils recited in front of people. Even worse, Charles was signed up to take Reading Lessons, too. Helen and Doc were making him do it. Charles screamed and yelled and laid on the floor and kicked his feet. It didn't change Helen's or Doc's mind. He had to go, no matter what. Charles was kind of a spoiled kid. He got his own way lots of times, but … "tough toenails!" This time Helen told them it would do them both good, maybe make little gentlemen out of them. You had to laugh when you thought about that, imagining how those two could ever be gentlemen. But maybe Mrs. Ada Mason might just do it!

Alice Ann was excited about it; Mrs. Thompson wasn't giving summer piano lessons and no more trombone lessons until school started. Learning how to memorize poems and then perform in front of people sounded like one way to someday be a movie star like Shirley Temple and Jane Withers!

Each Saturday morning they walked to Mrs. Mason's house, Ned and Charles and Alice Ann, carrying a quarter apiece to pay for their lessons. Charles and Ned had their lessons together; you could almost guess why. Then they could go on home and play armies in the backyard, using matchsticks for each army: red tops for Ned and blue tops for Charles. It was hard to understand how they could play in the dirt for hours with only matches and rocks and twigs (for trees, Ned said). They jabbered all the time, about who was winning the battles and taking turns, losing.

Real life was much more important. Right now it was learning as much as you could about everything to do with performing. It was fun to walk with a book on your head and sit down without plopping and, most of all, to speak distinctly. Alice Ann loved the word:

distinctly. It had a grown-up sound, and she would use it someday in everyday talk.

The first poem (Mrs. Mason called them "readings") to learn was "The Fairie Queen," and Alice Ann had it almost learned by heart after she and Mrs. Mason read it through five times. The half-hour zipped by like ten minutes, and it was suddenly time to walk home, saying the lines all the way until she got to town and there were people on the sidewalk looking funny at her talking to herself. "Someday," she thought with a smile, "they'll remember me after I'm a famous Hollywood star in the movies and they'll say how they saw me rehearsing while I walked down Main Street." It was a sensationful thought to hug to yourself all the way to the studio.

She could tell one person about it; that was Gwen. For sure the best thing about having relatives was being lucky enough to have girl cousins. They could be like best friends, only if they lived closer. Gwendolyn lived in the country, on a farm, but so many miles away that she went to a one-room country school with all the grades together and bathrooms in little beat-up shacks with Monkey Ward catalogs for toilet paper.

Saturdays Gwen came into town with her folks, and they almost always came by the studio since her dad, Uncle Romey, was Daddy's brother. They never stayed long, since Saturday night was a real busy time at the studio. Customers were always coming to get their photos or rolls of film developed in the darkroom.

Once Alice Ann took Gwen into the darkroom to show her how Daddy developed film and printed and enlarged pictures. In another year, maybe when she was twelve, the photographer's daughter could do some of that work in the darkroom. It was another thing to look forward to and plan for; maybe when she was all grown up and Daddy wanted to spend more time fishing at the lake, then it would be keen to be in charge of Conger's Studio.

One thing she knew she would do different; Alice Ann would get pictures to people on time. She never said anything about it, but when it was her turn to do what was called "waiting on the front," she prayed that nobody would come in whose photos weren't ready yet. Her face got all red and her hands kind of sweaty when she had to tell Mrs. Kowalski that it would be two more days before her order was ready. Daddy had told Mrs. Kowalski it would be ready the day she came in, but Mother had to explain that he got behind in his work or, better still, he had to send for more folders from the folder company. Sometimes it seemed easier to say for them to wait a minute while she went back and checked with Daddy. Then she could say he was just now working on them and it would be maybe tomorrow before the order was ready. Alice Ann hoped it wasn't a big lie.

Already she was doing proofs. It was fun to put the negatives in the wooden proof boxes smack dab against the glass, always right side down, and then the proof paper against the negative to be held there while she screwed down the back cover. And the next step was to set the proof boxes out in the full sunshine on the front sidewalk. You needed to watch until the sunshine turned the paper kind of red; the trick was to grab the proof boxes out of the sun before it turned the paper black. If it did, you had to start all over again and waste that sheet of proof paper. Daddy didn't like waste.

There were some wasted papers when Alice Ann first started doing proofs. It didn't take her long, though, to figure out how far to count: "One-thousand-one, one-thousand-two, one-thousand-three," and so on until the sun's fading was just the right darkness and the proofs were ready for customers to look at them and choose which pose they liked the best, before everyday light faded them completely. The proofs needed to be put into brown envelopes the minute they were made. Alice Ann was careful about that, and Daddy was proud, she could tell.

Ned wanted to watch her proofing, but having someone there fidgeting was enough to make a person nervous. Sometimes out there in front of the studio, Mr. Gzehoviak walked by, and she waited until he got past before she started. It was important to get the proofs perfect, since Daddy was what Mother called a "perfectionist." He'd gone to photography college in Illinois to learn how to be the very best kind of photographer.

Maybe that's what Alice Ann would do someday. That is, if Mother would change her mind about wanting her daughter to be a teacher, like she'd been and *her* mother had been. Maybe she could be a photographer *and* a teacher. Grown-ups' plans were so hard to change. It was easier to just go along with them most times. When you were twelve or thirteen, it might be better to speak your mind. As long as you kept smiling along with it.

There came a day when Daddy decided that Alice Ann was tall enough to try taking a photograph with his studio camera. She was almost as tall as Daddy, because he wasn't a tall man. His nickname that Harv O'Brien used was "Stub." Grandma C. said he was short because of a sickness as a little boy. It made his legs stop growing as long as they should've.

Maybe Daddy got tired of her asking when she could take a photo with the big camera. On a Sunday when the studio front door was closed to customers, he told her it was time to try. But what to take a picture of? Jane Ellen was down for her nap, and Ned was off playing with Charles. There was a vase with flowers on the dining room table. Aunt Belle had brought them from her garden. Would they do?

Daddy looked at the vase Alice Ann was holding, smiled and said, "Yes, it would make a good still life." He brought out the table he used for First Communions and put the lace cloth over it. All the time she was wondering why it was called "a still life." Even if the flowers weren't connected any more to the ground, they weren't dead yet. They were *still living,* for a bit, so they were "still life." Alice Ann thought about asking Daddy, but didn't. Daddy wasn't one to talk a lot; when Ned asked questions or went on and on about something he thought was important, Daddy would always say, "Don't be mouthy." She knew what it meant. When things had to be said, Mother mostly did it. And Daddy never called her "mouthy."

It wasn't easy to keep still when Daddy brought out the wooden film case and showed her how to slip it into the slot in the camera's side, to expose the negative that could be used to print a photograph of the vase. Then Daddy twisted the big wheel on the side to move the camera down lower and pushed a lever to keep the camera's traveling wheels tight against the floor. Then he explained how to move into position under the black cloth and pull out the metal protective shield away from the film, and to look straight ahead at the screen where she saw the vase of flowers and the table with the cloth, but it was all upside down!

There had to be a good reason, and Daddy told her before she could ask. It was because of the table being a reflection in a mirror that was inside the camera. Or something like that. Too busy looking and turning the control knob back and forth to make the table blurry and then sharp-looking, and hearing Daddy's voice sounding like he was talking to a grown-up made her lose track of all that he was saying. When the picture was what Daddy called "in focus," he handed her the little black bulb she'd seen him use often. She squeezed it like he said to, and the image of the vase on the table blinked. Alice Ann thought she'd taken her first photo, but no. She had to keep her thumb upon a metal knob attached to the black bulb and then push it down at the same time she squeezed the bulb. Wow! It was more complicated than it looked. But once she understood how, Alice Ann concentrated, looking at the upside-down view, pushing down the knob and squeezing the bulb at the same time.

Daddy said that now there should be a photograph on the exposed negative. He pulled out the wooden negative holder and put another one into the camera "just for good measure." This time he moved the camera nearer to get a "close-up shot" of the flowers and had to re-focus. Alice Ann nodded, feeling grown up and special, knowing what that meant.

She was so happy and proud that when they took the holder into the darkroom for developing the negative, she talked a blue streak. She told Daddy how Aunt Netta had told her that the reason Daddy went to Photography College in Effingham, Illinois, was because he saved five cars from burning up in a storage barn. They had belonged to a real rich man in the town where Daddy as a young World War I veteran was working. When the barn caught on fire, Daddy ran home for the gas mask he'd brought with him from France,

ran into the barn wearing it. He drove each car out, and the man was so grateful he sent Clayton Conger to any college he chose.

There in the darkroom, developing the negatives beside Daddy, Alice Ann was so proud and she told him so. All Daddy said was, "Aunt Netta gabs a lot. There were only three cars."

* * * * * * * * * *

Everybody said it was the hottest summer since the Depression and drought. Those two bad times seemed to go together whenever people talked about troubles. They especially worried about the farmers' crops. If the farmers in Sherman County didn't have good crops in their fields, they didn't spend their money for studio photos. Thinking back, Alice Ann recalled some of long

119

ago "hard times." She must've been pretty little when she sat on the packed hard dirt of the backyard, thinking if they were rich, then they'd have soft green grass and tall trees for shade and lovely flowers like in Aunt Belle's garden.

The Liberty Theatre was the only cool place in town. It had a sign out front alongside the Coming Attractions. It said "water-cooled interior." There was a giant metal tank on top of the Liberty, filled up with water that got mixed up somehow with the air inside to cool everyone in the seats. Ned and Alice thought how nice it would be to live in the Liberty in the summer. They would always be cool, watching all the picture shows over and over. Maybe they wouldn't watch *all* day; they'd play out in the lobby some of the time, and help out by picking up the candy wrappers and scraping gum off the seat bottoms.

Ned really got into the idea, but she knew it was what Daddy called "only a pipe dream." Their only cool place was on the linoleum under the dining room table. They spread out in underpants and bare feet. Mother hung wet towels in the window where the curtains had been, and they lay on their tummies on the shiny cool floor, talking about the picture shows at the Liberty.

Alice Ann reminded Ned of when he thought that the Metro-Goldwyn Mayer lion lived in the Liberty basement. He was real little when she first began taking him to Saturday matinees. Sometimes he could sit through the whole movie without twitching too much. Ned especially liked the beginning of any picture show that had the Metro-Goldwyn-Mayer lion up there, growling and turning his head sideways. Ned did love that lion. Later on, it embarrassed him when Alice Ann told about when he was really little and thought the lion lived in the Liberty's basement. Daddy got Sal Slominski to take them downstairs and examine all the corners. (Sal called them nooks and crannies, and he could've laughed about it, but he didn't.) Ned was kind of satisfied the lion wasn't there right then, but he always wanted to go down again to see if maybe it came back.

Sal Slominski was one of those adults who took little kids seriously. He brought out his flashlight that he used to take people to their seats after the show had started and it was hard to see. Sal flashed the light into all the nooks and crannies, behind big storage boxes and 'way under the stairs. Ned walked home a little sadly that day. He had been so sure he'd see the lion.

Alice Ann then began thinking that there might not be as much magic in the world as she and Ned had always believed there was. To find out that grown-ups always had explanations for mysterious things wasn't the best, somehow. It was part of growing up, she decided. But Ned was still too young to hear that. He wouldn't like the feel of emptiness, like she did just thinking about it. Little kids should believe in magic as long as they could.

GROWING UP CAN GET YOU MATURITY

It seemed ages before her legs were strong enough and also long enough to go upstairs to Daddy's frame-making room and help him. Ned still had to stay down on step number four, and he pretended to be happy lining up toy town and cars and stuff. Alice Ann got to dust in the frame-room and pick up all the little wood scraps that Daddy whittled off; then she watched him sitting on his stool kind of half-hidden in a black-painted box on legs with a glass-covered empty square with a bright light showing upwards from down below. Daddy used a teeny pointed pencil, making teeny-tiny dots on negatives where faces were pimply or wrinkled or frowny. When the photographs were printed, people were happy with how very nice they looked. Except for old Mrs. Maciejski, who told Daddy she'd earned those wrinkles and didn't want even one taken off!

Upstairs was a wonderful place, kind of dark and spooky when the sun didn't shine through the only window there at the head of the stairs. She could sit on the top step and look down on Aunt Belle's house and Uncle Ashley trimming his hedge. Mr. Gziehoviak might come strolling along or Mrs. Copperfield carrying groceries. Once when the window was open with no screen, a pigeon came and sat there on the sill, and Alice Ann could have reached right out to touch him.

One of the best things to do upstairs was watch Daddy cut lengths of painted wood, fit them together, and nail them into different sizes of beautiful frames for pictures. Where the wooden corners came together, he used matching colored paint to fill in the coming-together crack, so that when the frames were done, they looked like they'd been carved out of one piece of wood. It was something Daddy had learned at Effingham Photography College in Illinois.

With the frame lying face-down, he would fit a piece of glass into the grooves, next the picture, face down, too, so it would show through the glass. The cardboard that was fitted in next was called the "backing," Daddy said. Next he wet a long brown strip of tape to hold the backing onto the frame. The last step was attach-ing what he called eye-screws ever so carefully to the frame for holding the woven wire that would hang the picture on the wall. It took a long time to get all that done. Maybe when she was big, Alice Ann could help frame.

One not-to-be-forgotten day, Daddy brought a framed picture downstairs and laid it on the floor. He asked how would Alice Ann like to clean the glass? She'd seen Mother do it dozens of times, with Bon Ami and a clean cloth, wetting the cloth and sprinkling it with Bon Ami, then onto the glass in big white circles, until it was all covered, waited for it to dry and then took another clean cloth to wipe away the Bon Ami.

Alice Ann knew every step to it. Mother already had the wet cloth ready. The picture inside the frame was a beautiful white horse with mane floating like a cloud behind him; Alice Ann thought of it hanging on someone's wall and people saying, "Doesn't Mr. Conger do a wonderful framing job?"

She bent carefully over the frame, trying not to tremble, because she felt so special to be doing the Bon Ami. But the next thing that happened was so quick and so awful she couldn't think straight about it. Somehow her knee resting on the frame slipped onto the glass before she could pull it back! The terrible crunching sound was one she'd never forget. Not in a million years. The look on Mother's face wasn't good, either.

What happened then was Daddy patting her shoulder before he picked up the picture and carried it back upstairs to start all over again. Alice Ann couldn't watch him; she covered her eyes, but pretty soon uncovered them and sat very quiet on the davenport by the window. The studio was so quiet. After a long while, Daddy came back with the horse picture and new glass. In her mind, she saw him doing all the work again, and she was so very ashamed and bashful. She got ready to watch Mother do the cleaning of the glass.

But right then Daddy asked, "Are you ready to try again, Diddy?" That was the name Ned had for her when he was too little to say "sister." It was a funny name. Alice Ann wasn't sure she liked it, but this time when Daddy said it, she loved it. He hadn't called her that for a long time. She took the wet rag and the Bon Ami and started the job. She'd never forget this day in a million years. And she knew that she had the very best daddy in all the world.

* * * * * * * * * *

Her name was Harriet, like Mother's, but she sparkled. Her hair sparkled like Shirley Temple's, and her fingers did the same when she waved them. Her eyes sparkled with what Mother called "enthusiasm." Alice Ann tried walking like Harriet, moving her shoulders sideways each time she took a step. But her dancing was the most sparkling. In the *Sherman County Times* she advertised what she called a "review." It was just before the Saturday matinee at the Liberty. Alice Ann and Ned always went, but this time they went early to see the review.

Harriet Hyde tap-danced as good as Shirley Temple, and then she twirled and dipped like Ginger Rogers. Alice Ann couldn't breathe, it was that beautiful. Then Harriet Hyde took off her tap shoes and put on slippers with ties round the ankle. She danced with the music on her tippy-toes. The clapping was like thunder. And after the double-feature, you got to go down to the basement and sign up for what she called "tryouts." She said she would give dancing lessons so that you could dance just like she did!

Ned said he didn't want dancing lessons. Boys don't dance, he said, even when Alice Ann reminded him of Mickey Rooney and Fred Astaire. Ned reminded Alice Ann that Mother would have to give permission. By then it was almost suppertime, so they hurried home, Alice Ann praying all the way that Mother would come back to the Liberty with her.

This once, her prayers were answered. Mother said, "Yes-it-might-be-good-for-you-if-it-doesn't-cost-too-much."

When they reached the Liberty basement, kids were lined up against the wall and Harriet Hyde was stopping in front of each one, doing a step she called the Waltz Clog. She had each girl and boy try to copy the step she did. Since Alice Ann was at the very end of the line, she watched each time, practicing in her head just how to do it. Harriet told them to use their whole bodies in the step, loose like a rag doll dancing. By the time it was Alice Ann's turn, she could do it almost as well as Harriet herself. It was something to remember when she was famous in Hollywood, that her first try-out was so very good. Harriet Hyde told Mother, "Here is talent, Mrs. Conger, Your daughter is a natural."

The bad news was that dancing lessons from a professional were 'way too much for Daddy to afford, no matter how natural Alice Ann was. There wasn't enough money. Kids like Ellen Amick and Margery Smith got signed up that very night. Alice Ann understood; she really did. The lessons were something too good to dream or even pray about. She'd kind of known it all along. She'd never get to Hollywood and be a dancing star.

That night in bed Alice Ann could hear Mother and Daddy talking in the kitchen about the lessons. They talked a long time and she couldn't go to sleep, trying to listen. When sleep came, she dreamed about pulling the Keep Smiling sign down from Daddy's camera, but then being followed by it all around the studio … keep smiling … keep smiling. When she was a little kid, she had believed it was a kind of special message to her, but now there wasn't a whole lot to smile about.

It wasn't in the dream, though, that Harriet Hyde came to the studio next day, sparkling away and asking to see "the Boss." That meant Daddy, and when he came, Alice Ann walked slowly from the front of the studio toward the kitchen. She heard something that stopped her. Harriet Hyde wanted her photograph taken by Conger's Studio and would give Alice Ann dancing lessons in return for three 8 x 10s, four 5 x 7s, and a dozen wallet size, plus tinting for all but the wallets. Wonder of wonders, she heard Daddy saying yes, he guessed he could do it.

Lessons were Monday and Wednesday, and rehearsal with all the kids on Saturday morning. It would all happen at Uncle John Galloway's furniture store over on Main street. For sure, it was the happiest time of Alice Ann's life. What made her even happier was Harriet Hyde's announcing that after all the lessons, there would be a dance program for the public. It would be called "Alice in Wonderland."

Something hard to believe was when Alice Ann was chosen to be the Alice. Was it because of her name? Or her hair that was now down to her shoulders this summer? Maybe it was because she learned all the steps frontwards and backwards, remembering to think of being a rag doll moving with the music. Too excited to sleep at night, Alice Ann planned her trip to Hollywood to be a moving picture star alongside Shirley Temple. No one would ever believe the sweet, golden feeling she had all over her body. It made her look into the bathroom mirror a lot, to see if there was the sparkle like Harriet Hyde's. Inside and out, she felt sparkly. Walking with her shoulders moving from side to side made Ned call her a "prissy priss," so she stopped.

When Daddy took the photographs of Harriet Hyde, she was wearing a beautiful blue dress with her initials H H, embroidered on the stand-up collar. Alice Ann got to see the proofs when they were ready for Harriet to decide which pose was best.

Rehearsals were hard when some kids didn't know their steps or were sick and didn't come. Alice Ann prayed not to be sick. On the day to pick up her finished photos, Harriet Hyde brought a pattern for Mother to use in making the Alice in Wonderland costume, blue with a ruffly white apron and big bow. Also, there would be little blue bows on her tap-shoes. It was all so exciting it almost made a stomach ache start.

When only a few days were left before the dance program, Jo Ann and Margery and Alice Ann went early to rehearsal; the door to the furniture store was locked. They waited. Finally Uncle John Galloway came and told them to go on home. He looked very stern. Then he said there would be no rehearsal. There would be no program. Harriet Hyde had "skipped out of town," not leaving a reason. Suddenly the stomach ache was there, all the way home, going to tell Mother the news and that she might just as well not finish the Alice in Wonderland costume.

* * * * * * * * * * *

The McGhyhy kids, Jaqueline and Richard, had a swell idea to have a club; they'd call it "The Alley Gang," copied from the funny papers and "Our Gang" picture show with Alfalfa and his pals. Jaqueline told Ned and Alice Ann, "We all live by the alley and we play in the alley and find swell things in junk cans and spy on ol' Mr. Haney in his skivvies. We'll have some special passwords that only we know to write messages and hold secret meetin's and ..." Jaqueline could go on and on once she got started, but it seemed like a good idea.

Alice Ann got to be door-keeper when they had their first meeting in McGhyhys' fruit cellar. Charles lived a block away, but he got to be a member since Helen promised to make cookies for them. They had to let Royce Watson join since he lived next door to McGhyhys and his grandma mixed a big batch of lemonade for the meeting.

Royce had allergies, so he always looked like he was crying. Some of the time he *was* crying, because he wanted his way all the time; he could turn on what Ned called "the water works" at the slightest thing. Jaqueline said he was afraid of his own shadow. Maybe not. He was just a little kid with skinny legs and a drippy nose that he never wiped. Alice Ann was glad Ned wasn't that way: snuffly and whiney and then stuttery when he was scared. Royce lived with his grandpa and grandma since his mom and dad weren't around. Nobody knew where.

At the next meeting Jaqueline was president and said no one who was a fraidy-cat should belong. That let Royce out. He cried a bit, but seemed to understand. Alice Ann felt sorry for him, and sorrier that he took the half-full-yet pitcher of lemonade back across the McGhyhys' driveway.

You wondered how long Royce would be a fraidy-cat. Would he grow up to be a scaredy big boy and then frightened-all-the-time man? When a big dog came down the sidewalk, Royce ran to his grandma's porch swing and hid behind it until the dog was gone. That made it a real surprise to see what Mother said was Royce "standing his own guard" with the Polish boys that day.

It happened because of Mrs. Johansen, the dough-nut lady, living across the street in a tumble-down house. She was fatter than even Daddy's Aunt Myrtle, but she made the best doughnuts in town. She wasn't Royce's aunt, but he called her his "Aunt Lydia" and took money over to buy six doughnuts almost every day. Mrs. Johansen's house always smelled delicious, but it was messy and worn out. The floor had a few boards missing, so you had to be careful stepping. The curtains were raggedy, but the kitchen was sparkly-clean; otherwise Mother would never have let them buy doughnuts or yummy doughnut holes that just fit into your mouth.

On the day that the circus would come to town, the Alley Gang was out in front of McGhyhys watching. Down the street were lots of people standing, too, and Royce was out there. Right out of the blue suddenly there were three tall Polish boys crowding them off the sidewalk and spitting all over it to show how tough they were. Then one of them pointed across the street and yelled for even people down the block to hear: "HEY! WOULDJA LOOK AT DAT UGLY OLD FAT LADY OVER DERE!" And there was Mrs. Lydia Johansen in her floppy slippers and her cooking apron smudged with flour, watching for the circus parade.

Before they knew what was happening, there was little Royce Watson running over to the Polish boy who said it. He put his hands on his hips, stuck his jaw out and shouted back in his biggest voice: "Th-th-that's no ugly big fat lady! That's OUR AUNT LYDIA!" Then, like a balloon that's losing its air, Royce seemed to get littler and paler and scaredy-looking again. He turned and sure as anything ran for his grandma's front porch to hide behind the porch swing.

The big boys laughed and hooted some, then walked on down the block. You could hear the calliope begin to toot down the street, but Jaqueline with the rest of the Alley Gang went up to Watsons' front porch and pulled Royce out. President Jaqueline said it was for sure a brave, brave thing he'd done , and they voted on the spot for Royce to be back in the club and bring the lemonade.

* * * * * * * * * *

In thinking about it, maybe boys were a necessary part of God's plan. Most boys were dopey or pests. That wasn't counting Ned or Charles or Paul. Brothers and cousins were different, because they were family. All boys would eventually grow up to be daddies or presidents or movie stars. Alice Ann had to keep remembering that Ken Maynard and Tom Mix were boys, too, once and possibly as bothersome.

Back in third grade, Billy Line had been bothersome. He'd backed her up against the wall and asked her to be his girl-friend. Saying "no" to him wasn't hard. She hadn't wanted to be anybody's girl-friend then. Billy was extra smart and might grow up to be a lawyer or principal. He already had the thick glasses to make his eyes seem big, and a double chin that bobbled over his collar when he was excited.

Charles was the first boy ever to kiss her. He was

not a blood cousin, but just as good, being Helen's and Doc's son. Ned and Charles played cowboys and Jack Armstrong in the Mohrs' backyard, and sometimes Alice Ann was included. Once when she was being rescued by Charles from bank robbers, he kissed her, right there in his tire swing. She smelled his bubble gum and his sweaty boy-smell, but she never told Mother. It was a special secret.

Mostly, she wanted Paul to kiss her just once, but the wanting never did any good even when they played Tarzan and Jane in his backyard that went all the way down to Dead Horse Creek. There were long grapevines to swing on; Paul was Tarzan and Ned played Cheetah, so Alice Ann got to be Jane, wishing there would be a time when Paul thought Tarzan should rescue her. He was always too busy with Ned, swinging on the vines and yelling the Tarzan yell. It was still a good time, especially after the Tarzan matinee when they'd get new ideas for adventures.

Back in fourth grade, Paul and Alice Ann performed in the school operetta, "Aunt Drusilla's Garden." They each had a solo and also sang together in a duet. Paul's voice wasn't strong like hers, so it was best for Alice Ann to sing softer than ordinary. Trouble was, when she did that, Paul sang even softer and you couldn't hear him.

The day came when she knew she couldn't marry Paul like she wanted to; they were first cousins, Aunt Netta reminded her, when the wish slipped out while they were doing dishes together. Times spent at Aunt Netta's were so friendly and gentle. Paul's mother was a lot like Daddy: quiet and smart. Well, after all, they were brother and sister. The same things made them laugh when they talked about being little kids together.

When Alice Ann and Paul were grown-ups, they would laugh about playing Tarzan and Jane at Dead Horse Creek. One thing, she'd always love Paul. He was kind and handsome and could really yell like Tarzan.

The sixth grade boys were all dopey pests, especially Max Bennett. He sat in the desk behind her, and when she wore a dress with a sash tied in back, Max would untie it and wrap it around the front bar down below on his desk. It was embarrassing to try to get up and find out it wasn't possible. Before Miss Couch could look their way, Max undid the sash. But there it hung, dragging on the oily floor. She hated Max Bennett. She hated him so much that she told on him at recess. All that Miss Couch said was, "Now, Alice Ann, Max is doing it to get your attention. Boys are too shy to let you know they like you, so they do little tricks to make you notice them. You'll understand about it when you're older."

The next time it happened, Alice Ann swung around and shoved Max's arithmetic book off his desk with a loud thump. The whole sixth grade jumped, especially Max. Miss Couch was quick to turn from the blackboard; she walked down the aisle and saw Alice Ann's sash tied to Max's desk. Without saying a word, she pointed a long finger at it and waited until he unwrapped the sash. It was embarrassing to have all eyes on you, but there was some satisfaction (she liked that word) in seeing Max's face the color of a watermelon.

"Now, Alice Ann, would you like to move your things to the empty desk by the window where you won't be bothered?" What a relief! Somewhere she'd heard a saying about a thing being a "necessary evil," and she guessed that's what boys were. They were evil all right. But at least they would grow up and be husbands and daddies or presidents or movie stars.

* * * * * * * * * *

Looking backward in time, Alice Ann could recall only a few thoughts about her body and its different parts. There were parts that "just-aren't-talked-about-in-polite-company," as Mother said once with a frown. She couldn't understand why it bothered Mother when Alice Ann wrote "my hole" on the envelope with her incision pictures Daddy had taken for Dr. Weinberg. That's what it was. It must've meant something else to Mother. It was pretty plain that you didn't talk about going to the bathroom in polite company. Charles called it "peeing." Whenever somebody did, they laughed behind their hands. She wondered about it for a long time.

One day the Thomas girls took her out into the cornfield behind their house and said they had a secret she could NEVER never, EVER tell anybody, especially Mother or Daddy. Secrets were fun, so she went along, expecting some kind of special news like maybe Mrs. Thomas having a baby or even a divorce like Virginia's mom. But once they were deep into the big, tall cornstalks, Millie pulled down Alice Ann's panties and tickled her where she went to the bathroom. It felt kind of good, better than under your ribs or arm, but about that time Mother called from the Thomases' front porch where she was visiting Mrs. Thomas and said it was time to go home.

On the way, Mother asked, "What-was-going-on-out-there-in-the-cornfield?" and Alice Ann told a lie. It as so hard to look Mother in the eye and say, "Nothing, just looking at the corn," but she remembered she'd promised hope-to-die she'd keep the secret. Plus, how could she tell Mother something that was pretty certain to be "a thing-just-not-talked-about"?

Only two times before had she felt that same kind of nice, itchy feeling "down there." Once when she was very little, needed to go to the bathroom but was already in the tin bathtub. She was pretty little, but figured out that the yellow stuff she let out of her bottom would just get mixed in with all that bath water. So she did it, let it go, and got a nice tickling feeling down there. Alice Ann never did it again.

Later on, when she found out that Daddy and Ned stood up to do what they called "urinate," it seemed like something to do, also. It was difficult, finally pulling her panties completely off, since it stretched them too much when she straddled the toilet. Once in place, she had to kind of sit across the stool and look at the wall. It sure wasn't comfortable, but once she got the urine going, she felt the funny tickling down there, like before.

Once was enough to do it, like in the bathtub. It was just too much trouble for one little tickle. Besides, somehow she knew that Mother wouldn't like her to do it. If you shouldn't talk about it, then maybe you shouldn't do it.

Those times with that part of her body came back to Alice Ann, though, when in seventh grade Hygiene they found out all about Sex. Dr. Amick came to the school and took all seventh grade boys to the music room in the basement. Nurse Pichota stayed with the

girls and explained that she was there to talk about their bodies changing into grown-up women's. Wow! It was so exciting to finally hear someone speak about "things-just-not-talked-about." There was a little worry, too, that Mother would have some objections. But that was forgotten when Nurse Pichota began talking and showing charts.

Just like one of the chart's drawings, Alice Ann had the beginnings of breasts. They weren't very big, like Margaret Taylor's. Margaret was already in brassieres and sticking her chest out like a movie star. All the boys liked Margaret.

It got very interesting to hear about female vaginas, even with all the giggling. She was glad to know that she had one, down there where the tickling was, and it was good to know why she needed one. It was worth running all the way home at noon.

There was Mother at the ironing board in the doorway to catch any breeze that came along. She unplugged her iron and smiled. There was a good smell of warm custard. The sun shone through the new curtains she'd made. Everything seemed very bright and perfect. Alice Ann felt so bursting-out good that she said to Mother, "Guess what? **"I could have a BABY!"** It was all tied up with her periods she'd begun to have, but surely Mother knew that. It was a giant surprise to see Mother frown her mother-frown and spit out three loud words, each one stronger than the one before: **"YOU COULD NOT!"**

Hearing the words was such a shock that Alice Ann had to sit down, eat her sandwich, and not even taste the custard. She ran the six blocks to school, slowing down before she got there.

All the way she tried to understand Mother's reaction. After all, since there were three Conger kids, she and Daddy would've had to do the thing Nurse Pichota told them about. Of course, Mother had been pretty old before she had babies: twenty-six. Could it be that she thought you had to be real grown-up before getting pregnant? No, of course not. It was silly to imagine Mother being *that* dumb. She must have had a reason for saying what she did to Alice Ann, and kind of angry, too. It was embarrassing to look her or Daddy in the face at supper. And it was pretty clear that this was one of those "things-just-not-talked-about."

Now was definitely the time to stop being a little girl and start thinking about becoming a grown-up. From the information Nurse Pichota gave them, it had to do with knowing for sure what your body was becoming. Confusion came when Mother refused to talk about it. There was a way that she helped Alice Ann, though, without talking. She knew that her kids poked through the chifferobe drawers in the bathroom. They each had their own drawer: Jane Ellen's at the bottom where she could reach into it; next, Ned's all mishmashed with underpants and holey socks, Big-Little Books and rocks, not that fun to look through. Alice Ann's was above his, with her socks rolled up and panties folded with undershirts. It was easiest to reach, sitting on the toilet. She knew enough not to put anything in it that was secret, since she knew Ned must go through the drawers, too.

Her diary and pen-pal letters and Overland composition books stayed inside her desk where Ned was forbidden to look. He knew she was writing a book: MARJORIE MASON AT BOARDING SCHOOL, and sometimes he'd get to hear a chapter. But if the drop-leaf on the desk was closed tight, he was never to get into her things. Alice Ann could trust Ned.

Somehow Mother must have known that they inspected the drawers, because there on top of Mother's socks and nighties was a book that hadn't been there before. It was a small blue book: MOTHER TALKS TO MARY ELIZABETH, published by a Lydia Pinkham Health Products. Inside it were all the interesting things Nurse Pichota had told about — menstruation and ovaries and vaginas and pregnancy. Alice Ann already knew all it spoke of, but she figured it was good to be reminded. The one trouble was that she couldn't mention it to Mother, since then she'd know for sure that her chifferobe drawer was checked.

Waiting for Mother to bring out the book and discuss the things in it with Alice Ann was hard. It never happened. Maybe Mother was keeping the book so that she'd know all the Facts; or maybe she meant for Alice Ann to find it; she'd never know.

Seventh grade was by far the best grade, especially with Mr. Reynolds who was also principal. His office was next to grade seven, and sometimes he was in there talking on the telephone or punishing kids who misbehaved. That always meant they were "on your best behavior," as Mr. Reynolds put it, not knowing that all hell broke loose while he was gone. It was mostly boys who shot paper wads and yelled out the windows at little kids' recess, but sometimes the girls joined in. Alice Ann felt guilty going along with them, but there was a nice kind of scary feeling, being on the edge of disobeying, of being a part of the group that dared go against the rules. It was maybe a different part of being close to growing up, with a choice to go along with the crowd or not to follow. Having strict parents was kind of like being pulled tight into a box with the lid squishing you down into not moving.

Talking that over with someone helped; she sure didn't think it would be Ham, but he turned out to be an awfully good listener and said he felt the way she did sometimes. His real name was Eldon Russell Holmberg, and he wasn't what you'd call very popular. Back in sixth, they'd all started calling him "hamburger" out of his last name, but shortened it to "Ham."

Alice Ann and Ham mightn't have become friends if he hadn't got hit in the stomach with a softball out on the playground. He had to come in from recess to rest in Mr. Reynolds' office. That was the day she had the turn to answer the telephone and add attendance records for the office. Ham came in looking so pale and hurting that Mr. Reynolds had him lie down on the cot there while Mr. R. went back to umpiring the soft ball game.

When Alice Ann finished the attendance and was just sitting there, Ham started talking. He said, "I recall how back in fifth, you were the girl the town prayed for not to die." Ham told her how he was real sick once. He wasn't smarty like the other boys; in fact, Ham talked to her like they were buddies. It was nice the way the two of them kind of "clicked," like you saw in movies, but not like love-birds. It was different. She knew from school grades that Ham was smart, but he was more than that. He was intelligent, one of her favorite words now. He was easy to talk to, and he really listened to what you said, like it was important.

They compared growing up in a business place, Ham in his sister's cafe and she in the studio. Ham's folks were gone, and Ruby was raising him in a little house by the Baptist Church. Alice Ann thought about their getting to be friends in kind of an odd way, but she could tell that the two of them were something special. It wasn't even like in a boy-girl way, to her anyway. It seemed hard to explain to Ellen and Margery when they teased her about Ham hanging around like he sometimes did.

When they were in eighth grade, Ham asked her if she'd like to go to the Sunday matinee and then over to Ruby's Cafe for the best chili in town, and Alice Ann after a minute said, "Yes, Eldon, I'd like that," and never called him Ham again to his face.

* * * * * * * * * *

It was what she'd been waiting all summer to hear: "Alice Ann-grab-your-bathing-suit-we're-going-to-the-river-with-Harvey." There'd been no rain. The studio was hot. The backyard's dirt was packed hard. If only Aunt Belle had gone on vacation, they could sneak next door and sit under the shade and maybe climb the apple trees, or slide down the cellar door.

Now though, they could pile into Harv O'Brien's jalopy with the bread box filled with sandwiches and the thermos full of green Kool-Aid. It was a tight squeeze with Harv's and Daddy's fishing gear and towels and tablecloth. Ned and Jane sang out the window, "We're goin' t'th'rrr-river! We're going' t'th'river!" Alice Ann scooched down low so nobody would see her with such a rowdy bunch, but then happiness won out, and she sat up to join in the singing. Mother and Daddy smiled, not even worrying about the photos back at the studio, needing to be pasted in folders, a big pile of them. For now nothing was important but the swimming and supper at the river.

Since the farmers were using river water for irrigation, there were lots of sandbars in the river to run on and chase long-legged birds and pile sand into castles and dig out moats around them to fill up with water. Mother said "No" about going over to the deep swimming holes on the west bank. Alice Ann wished she could try wading over just to see how deep it was, but she knew the current was swift and might sweep you under and away before you knew it.

Daddy and Harv set catfish lines in the deep places and then went over to Bowman Lake to fish for bass. Ned and Jane Ellen played in the shallow water trying to catch tiny fish that nibbled their toes. With the box camera she'd brought in her towel, Alice Ann took snapshots of Mother on a bleached-out log and one of Ned covering Jane with sand. They had such fun.

When Daddy and Harvey came back early from the lake, toting their gear and unpacking food at the picnic table, she knew it was time to come out of the river. The fishermen hadn't spent enough time to get their hooks in the water, Mother said while she climbed up the river bank and toweled dry with the others.

Daddy's face looked kind of sad, maybe from not catching the old granddad bass that always got away. Harv didn't look happy either. Why, she asked, and Daddy wiped a tear from his eye with the tail of his shirt. What he said next was quiet and with kind of a shaking in his voice: "The Lonowski boy drowned in the deep end of the lake. He'd been under too long."

Remembering how the big kids swam in Bowman Lake, Alice Ann could only think of the photo of Lenny in his confirmation clothes, smiling and holding his white prayer book. Leonard Lonowski wasn't a kid she really knew, since he went to Catholic School, a block from Public. But he was still a boy who got up in the morning and ate his breakfast, put on his school clothes and worried about being late, like all other kids did. Now he wouldn't be doing them. He was drowned. Dead. Gone, like Bobby Burke's mother, like Grandma C. It was a big thing to turn over in your mind, a sad thing. But she didn't cry.

The only person she could get sad enough to cry about was Grandma C. whose funeral was long ago, when Alice Ann was only five years old. Stuck in her memory was Daddy crying at the Service. It was a long time before she forgave Grandma C.'s going away and making Daddy awfully sad for many days. One thing hanging over from that time was the decision never to let anyone shorten her name to just "Alice," since that was the name the grown-ups used talking about Grandma C.

People's dying was a thing to worry over. She wanted to write a poem about it, but couldn't find the right words. Nothing rhymed with "funeral," and "service" had only "nervous" to go with it, so she gave up. Anyway, poems should be about happy things. She would only write poems to make people smile.

By now three of Alice Ann's poems had been published where someone she didn't even know could read them. "I Like to Live" was in the *Omaha World Herald* and "Thanksgiving Day" in the *Sherman County Times* and "The Gold Rush" in *Wee Wisdom. The World Herald* paid her a whole dollar, but the others didn't. *Wee Wisdom Magazine* must go all over the country, since one day here came mail from a girl in Tennessee who asked her for some clothes for herself and her sisters. They were poor, without enough to eat sometimes. But somehow Emily had a copy of *Wee Wisdom* with Alice Ann's address.

Together, Mother and Alice Ann put too-small dresses and panties and socks in a box; oh, yes, and one of Mother's dresses like new, only she hated it. They sent it to Emily, and she wrote back a big thank-you. She said she liked Alice Ann's poem, and could she send some money next time for food. Daddy put his foot down then and said he had barely enough money to put food on their own table. Alice Ann did something in secret, then. In a letter explaining what Daddy said, she sent the *World Herald* dollar to Emily. It made her feel all warm inside. Maybe it was enough, because Emily never did write again.

There were other letters from kids in other states,

and she started a list of pen-pals to correspond with. Thank goodness none of them wanted clothes or money. They exchanged pictures and postcards from towns far away. It was swell.

* * * * * * * * * *

It was only the second time Alice Ann saw Mother cry. Something was happening that was to worry about, she guessed. Something pretty serious. Dr. Amick had sad eyes that didn't go with the always-smile he had. Grown-ups were such a puzzle. There was a thing going on that must be truly bad, and she wished they'd just tell her! Maybe it was about her feeling achey sick all over. Then came something called a "spinal tap" for finding out what her sickness was.

Getting a spinal tap was terrible, smashing sensation, kind of like if you took hold of your tummy and your backbone at the same time, then squeezed them together so they almost touched each other inside your body. That was how she thought of it, while pain didn't stop for ages. When it did, breathing was only gasping, along with a thumping headache. Alice Ann wished to go back into the foggy sleep she'd been in before.

Mother had begun the crying when Dr. Amick whispered in her ear; she kept it up when he walked over to Alice Ann and said in a kind of not-really-wanting-to voice: "Sweetie, you are sick with something called infantile paralysis or poliomyelitis. It's a disease we don't know much about, but we won't let it spread to any one else. The Congers will be quarantined here at the studio for a few weeks."

There were some other things he said, and she couldn't understand. Maybe it was because of her head aching so bad that his voice seemed far away. She didn't

145

remember Daddy hanging that thin, mosquito-net curtain between herself and everyone. When her hand reached out to touch it, there was no curtain.

"Curiouser and curiouser," she said to herself, like Alice in Wonderland. Was she now that same Alice, in a dream? But a dream where she ached all over from her head to her toes? A dream where Jane Ellen tried to talk to her and Mother shooed her away? Where Dr. Amick began to be the White Rabbit in Wonderland? He was funny, standing there, taking her temperature and "tsk-tsk-tsk'-ing, then saying, "It's late, it's late," his whiskers shaking and his head nodding.

Alice Ann lay back on her pillow, but then decided to fly around the room in her dream. Looking down, she saw Ned and Jane Ellen at the supper table in the kitchen. She floated easily into the bathroom and then to the darkroom where Daddy was lifting negatives from the last pan and toting them to the wash tank. Then Mother was telling her to fly down and drink some water. Alice Ann was having too much fun, so she smiled at Mother and went back into the dream to find her diary and write down all the things happening. Whatta y'know? Her desk was moved, and a cot was there instead, with someone sleeping on it. Everything was dark except for moonlight coming in the window. She was back in bed, and the hurting in her back told to lie still, very still. Back and forth, it was daytime again and nighttime too soon, so she still was dreaming, she guessed.

There was the smell of Absorbine, Jr., the medicine Daddy used after playing ball with the Legion team. Mother rubbed it all over Alice Ann's legs and arms and chest and back, but the aching didn't go away. Soon,

Mother put big bath towels in hot water, as hot as her hands could stand. She wrapped the towels around wherever the pain was, and no more Absorbine, Jr. Thank goodness! Every night Mother got up from her cot and wrung out the hot towels to wrap them again around the aching legs and arms.

After awhile the dreams of flying went away. Dr. Amick told them that her fever had broken, so now she should be getting all well again! What she'd thought was a couple of days turned out to be three weeks of having infantile paralysis. Alice didn't like calling her sickness infantile paralysis. It sounded too much like a baby, an infant. And how ever did she get it? Dr. Amick said she was the only one in the whole county who had it, but there were other polio cases in the state and in other states, too.

Mother said there'd been signs on the front door and back fence warning people to stay away from the contagious area. "Contagious" was a new word, but Alice Ann didn't think she'd use it after this was all over. Would it be over soon? Time went so slow; she could write in her diary, but not send letters to anyone yet. Relatives and friends sent get-well cards and letters. Ellen wrote the best letters, telling about high school and how swell it was to be a freshman.

Thinking back to the first day of school made her sad. Mother had made her a new dress of her favorite color: green. It seemed so exciting to be finally entering high school. It was like a picture show flashing inside her head: that extra-special day when her headache wouldn't go away while she knelt down to see Brownie's new puppies in the backyard. Brownie was the dog they'd rescued at Bowman Lake, and her new puppies were wriggly and cute with eyes still shut.

What had been strange then was the way Alice Ann couldn't stand back up once she'd squatted down by the doghouse. Her legs just wouldn't work right, so Daddy had to come help her up. She didn't want to be late for first-morning classes.

"Alice Ann-you-best-stop-at-Dr.-Amick's-clinic-before-you-go-on-to-school." Mother had said it when they trooped out the door. It had been too exciting to even eat breakfast, so that was why her head felt light and floaty, Alice Ann kept thinking. Maybe she had a little fever. Mother's face was stern. It crossed her mind not to stop at the clinic, just go on up the street to high school from the corner by the library where Ned and Jane Ellen left her. What if Dr. Amick sent her back home? Oh, no, he wouldn't on the very first day of high school! But the nurse after the examination said, "Go home." Darn that old nurse! Darn that nurse! Darn Mother! Darn poliomyelitis!

She wrote it in her diary before she got so very sick:

"It all seems like a horrible bad dream — my having poliomyelitis. It seems like in a few minutes I'll wake up and Jane Ellen and I will start to school on the first day in our new dresses. But we won't, because today is the last day of the first week, and I might not even be a freshman this semester. It makes me downright mad, and if I thought cussing would help, no one could stand being around me!

"With Mother cutting a little door through the wall into Daddy's darkroom from the pantry off the kitchen, Ned and Jane can get into the Big Room without bothering me. It's tough on Ned, but he pretends it's a secret passageway for an underground railroad. Yesterday he

put up a quarantine sign on the doghouse! The pup-
pies are so cute; Jane brings them in one at a time. Their
tails are starting to wag. We can't see Daddy. He comes
to the back gate and hands Mother mail, papers and
groceries. He's staying in Doc's basement, you know.
Helen came to talk over the fence and find out from
Mother what he should and should not eat. He'll stay
away for two weeks; the studio must be locked and there
won't be any business. This is the time of year when if
we ever have any business we have it now. I could just
bite somebody! When kids coming from the corner go
by, we hear them call out, 'Hold your breath and run
like lightning!' Mother says people cross to the other
side of the street so they don't come close to us."

Alice Ann didn't write down everything she was feeling, in case somebody would read her diary some-day. It took awhile to even write words that made sense, but she should keep some kind of record, in case she died. People did die of polio, right? She was glad she'd minded Mother, going to the clinic. If she hadn't stopped there, the whole high school might've been contaminated.

One good thing, though, was not having to be put in the hospital this time she was sick. She wondered if Daddy ever got all the hospital bills paid for double p., such a scary thing that she never asked. When she was little and heard "money is tight," she'd thought up the last dollar bill they had all wadded up and tight in Daddy's hand, waiting to go for food or stove oil. Wor-rying was a private thing that she did not write about in her diary. But with the fever dreams, she'd some-times wake up crying about not having enough money to get well from poliomyelitis. Part of the crying came from inside-the-bones aching, mostly down her back and along her legs. It didn't stop, but sometimes slowed down with the hot wet towels that Mother wrapped around the achings.

The night that the dreams stopped, she felt sweaty all over, but could think and talk straight, sit up to drink her soup and gobble the wonderful custard Mother made. Dr. Amick said, with his same sad-eyes smile, "Well, sweetie, the worst is over, I think. Now, stand up for me."

Mother helped swing Alice Ann's leg over the side of the bed to stand, kind of woozy, but fresh again right side up. "Now take a step for me." Dr. Amick held out his hands, too far to reach. The strangest thing happened! When she moved her right leg, it swung off to the side and backwards. She was like a puppet with a leg that needed strings to pull it down to the floor for walking. The doctor caught her leg and put her foot on the floor, saying, "Try the left leg, Alice Ann."

She gritted her teeth and took an enormous breath. Then when she moved the left leg, golly sakes! The same thing happened with it as with her right. There was no way to control it, no matter how hard she tried! It too hung loose and limp like a Raggedy Ann doll's. Her legs were sound asleep, but not tingling or even aching. What was wrong? Without even trying to wipe away her tears that kept coming, Mother and Dr. Amick put her back into bed.

Aunt Netta came and brought her special duck soup, but tears spilled into the soup while she sat in bed, trying to be happy that the worst was over, but knowing maybe it wasn't.

When you were a little kid, the worst thing that

could happen to you was getting run over by a truck and killed before you found out what it was like to grow up. By the time you were fourteen, dying was still the worst thing to happen. Lucky for Alice Ann, she didn't die twice when she could've.

Lying in bed again for so long made her think long and hard. Maybe it was "all in the cards" like Grandpa C. said, but he was just trying to make her feel better. He was good at that, with so many jokes that sometimes he forgot he'd told them to you twice, maybe three times. "How many wells does it take to make a river?" he'd ask. Before you answered, he'd say, "One, if it's deep enough!"

Grandpa C. came from Grand Island on the bus the minute they were out of quarantine. He said the Old Soldiers' Home could get along without him for awhile. He walked six blocks from Aunt Netta's each morning to tell Alice Ann his latest story. His "in the cards" thing started her thinking. Maybe being sick *was* part of The Plan. Not to argue with God about it, sometimes she prayed to be strong again, to walk and run and dance. Spending your life in a wheelchair could be different from what she really wanted: just to be a regular kid again, not a glamorous movie star nor to run faster than anyone or be smarter than most. It would be enough to be back like she was before, able to move her legs. That would be enough.

Depending on others to push you around wherever you wanted to go was a worry she tried to push away from thinking about. But before she could help it, Alice Ann had this image of herself sitting in a wheelchair with a blanket over her legs that didn't work. Her hands were folded tight together, and she had an old lady's look on her face, with a shawl over her shoulders. At night in dreams the awful picture came to her, with Daddy's "Keep Smiling" sign floating above her.

Dr. Amick made the nightmare picture go away. He told them that since it was too expensive for her to go to Warm Springs, Georgia, where President Roosevelt went for physical therapy, he'd made arrangements to admit Alice Ann into the Children's Orthopedic Hospital in Lincoln. It was all settled that she should go there to learn to walk again.

There wasn't even a "maybe" in his voice this time. He was talking like that's what would happen: walking, running, marching in band, being a freshman and going to classes, catching up with studies, doing gym, school dances even. Dr. Amick, bless his buttons, made all the difference with "what's in the cards." If there was some way to teach her legs to move the way they should, it could be at the Orthopedic Hospital. That wheelchair dream was gone forever.

No matter how much she wanted it, Dr. Amick said she must not sit up in Doc's car to go to Lincoln. They took out the back seat and laid an ironing board Alice Ann could lie upon. The trip took two days, so they stopped at Uncle Art's farm for the night, but Alice Ann was too excited to sleep. She stayed awake all night, listening to the quiet country sounds and then the rooster announcing it was time to get up and going.

Blanket wrapped around the ironing board helped. It was still a long, bumpy ride to the Orthopedic Hospital. "Alice Ann-you-must-lie-perfectly-straight-to-keep-back-and-legs-from-curling-up," Mother said, turning around many times to make sure Dr. Amick's orders were being followed. It was necessary.

To keep her mind busy, she closed her eyes and tried to remember nice things before the poliomyelitis struck. She recalled believing it was just the flu or a summer cold that made her skin hot and then cold. It started the night of the carnival on Main Street, with flashing lights and scary rides and cotton candy and gobs of people. She'd worn her best summer dress that Ellen said looked grown up. They rode the Tilt-a-Whirl and screamed bloody murder when their skirts flared up. Eldon followed behind them and asked Alice Ann to go on the ferris wheel, but she said, "No." He threw baseballs at the painted clown face and won a dinky toy dog she'd give to Jane.

Something strange had happened just before going home, now that she thought about it. The smells and sounds all came back: hot buttered pop corn, sawdust on the ground, merry-go-round music, men yelling numbers in the Bingo Tent. And all the people filling the streets, bumping, laughing too loud. Suddenly Ellen wasn't around and she went looking for her by the ferris wheel. Standing close to the heavy wire guard strung around the ride was the kid who ran it, whistling and smiling friendly-like. Alice Ann watched the seats as they moved down and around, wondering if Eldon had taken someone else, maybe Ellen. Then out of the blue, the young man operating the ferris wheel came over close to where she stood. He grinned and she smiled back. Then he asked, "Hey, honey, y-got th' time?"

For a minute she had thought he was one of the older high school boys, but in that moment he looked strangely even older. She held up her wrist to show him she didn't wear a watch; she didn't know the time. He turned away quickly to throw the switch for the ferris wheel to stop.

Ellen and Margery and Lois came by right then with double-decker ice cream cones, one for her, too. They teased her about flirting with a "carny guy." When Alice Ann told them what he'd asked, they whooped and screamed, *"Dummy!*

Dontcha know what he *meant?"*

As far as she could tell, all he meant was could she tell him the time. She had suddenly felt very uncomfortable then, enough to decide it was time to hurry home to the studio.

Remembering it while she lay on the ironing board going to Lincoln, she decided the carny guy was asking something else. She was glad to know they were near the hospital, so there were other things to think about.

Entering Lincoln, Mother took Dr. Amick's map from her pocketbook, directing Daddy down 10th Street to South Street, and a left turn. The Orthopedic Hospital should be there.

Good thing Mother was a "take-charge" person; she told them that she'd begun to be that, 'way back when she was nine and her own mother had rheumatic fever. She made the bread and bossed her brothers and sister. They called her "Ott."

She was the one deciding to take Alice Ann to the hospital's back entrance, after seeing many steps going to the big front door. There was no way to carry the ironing board up all those steps. Daddy drove to the alley and then the basement entrance. Mother found two men in white called orderlies, and they brought a shiny metal stretcher on wheels to slide her onto in nothing flat. From the basement it was up to 2nd floor in the elevator. A nurse rolled Alice Ann to what was the "Little Girls' Ward," and Mother went to fill out papers in the office.

Alice Ann suddenly saw how out of place Daddy looked, with his hat in his hands, standing like a little boy in a strange place, all shy and worried. When it was time to say good-bye, his face got red and splotchy. Mother took his hand and said they would go now to Clarissa's house to stay for a few days.

When Alice Ann was alone in a bed smelling of strong Clorox, two girls came over to say hello. Norma had crutches and only one leg. Juanita was in a wheel-chair with bandaged legs.

"You the new girl? Whatcher name?"

"You too big fer Li'l Girls' Ward. Gonna have pins betcha."

"Not leetle peens! *Beeg* ones!"

"They'll scrub yer head w' tar soap t'git out the' lice bugs."

"Y're onny here til there's a free bed on Big Girls' Ward."

"Charla dyin'. Nen, y'git 'er bed. How long y' stay?"

"Norma bineer two years almos'. Me, ah got burnt in fire."

"Downa hall, polio girl's got stay-out sign onna door."

"How come y'don' talk much? You skeered?"

Suddenly she was. Scared … achey … tired out … homesick. Pulling the sheet over her head helped. It blocked out the two girls who probably only wanted to be friends. She didn't want any right now. Did Mother forget to pack her diary? What was tar soap? Could she wear her own clothes? Why would beeg pins be put in her legs? How long would she be here? It all made her head spin. Dr. Amick was so sure that coming here would help her walk again. Was it "in the cards" like Grandpa C. said?

Things did work out for her not having to spend even one night in Little Girls' Ward. Charla who was dying must've been moved from Big Girls' the same day Alice Ann came, because after supper trays a nurse came with the stretcher on wheels. It hurt like crazy to be rolled onto the hardness, then go bumping down the hall to a bigger room. A kind-looking nurse named Trulla eased her into a bigger bed with even a softer pillow.

Trulla was Official Night Nurse, she told Alice Ann. She sat down by the bed and slid a bedpan under it for "Nightpee." Nurse Trulla treated her like a big sister would; that was so nice. And already knowing about bedpans was a comfort. Before "tinkling" (that's what Nurse Trulla called it), Alice Ann heard the funny saying the nurse always said when she brought bedpans to everyone in Big Girls. She said it so very fast, that Alice Ann made her say it slowly in order to copy it in her diary. Still, she rattled it off fast:

"Will-ya-wontcha-can't-I-coaxya-won't-cher-Maw-letcha-aw-c'mon-kidja-saidja-would!" Alice Ann said it slowly when all the lights were turned off at nine-thirty. You knew that Nurse Trulla was just down the hall at the Nurses' Station and it was fun to lie there, listening to traffic going by outside the windows 'way into the night on and on. Car lights turning the corner would flood the room's walls and light up spaces above some beds with get-well cards and family pictures tacked up. Above her bed she'd seen a ragged snapshot of a dog sitting by a mailbox. Somehow Charla had missed it when the other things were down, since it hung, almost hidden by the bed's metal headpiece. Lying on her stomach, she, Alice Ann, could see it drooping there, held with a bent safety-pin.

Someday I'll write a poem about it," she thought. "I'll get more pins, too, and hang it right side up for Charla." A big tear came in her eye and pretty soon more; she didn't know why. Then Nurse Trulla on her soft nurse's shoes came to wipe her face and pat her shoulder.

Redella was her name, but she made everybody call her "Rickets." That's what was wrong with her and why she was at the Orthopedic. Alice Ann kind of worried that she'd be called "Polio," but two other girls there were in the same boat.

Rickets talked to Mother when she visited; Daddy had gone back home. Staying at Clarissa's clear across the city made Mother get to Orthopedic by lunchtime, since she walked the two miles to save bus fare for bad weather days. She'd buy a sandwich from the drugstore across the street and sit by Alice Ann's bed while all the sick girls ate. Once she brought an orange for Rickets, only she called her "Crickets" or Redella. Her face got all sorry-looking when she spoke about her, but Rickets was such a happy person, it was hard to feel sad for her. Most days she wheeled herself around in a wheelchair, turning corners on one wheel and almost running into the nurses, who laughed.

When Mother came, she told all the news of back home, since she talked on the telephone every night with Daddy and Ned and Jane. It was still a mystery about where Alice Ann had picked up the "bug." Mother had her own ideas of where she got it. In other parts of the country that had polio outbreaks the doctors traced them to swimming pools. Remembering the two times they went to Ravenna and Kearney to swim, Mother decided to blame those places. What a nice change from the Loup River, they all thought, but maybe not so nice.

Alice Ann wrote letters back to the people who sent her get-well cards. She told about the Orthopedic, but didn't write down the sad things, like Lupey and Ruthie getting their bone scrapings, and Rickets' arms and legs so thin and white.

The first time Alice Ann heard Lupey's screaming and Ruthie whimpering like a puppy, Rickets explained what was going on. She'd seen it once when the nurses forgot to pull the curtain all the way. It happened once a week, the doctor and nurse coming with little curved knives to scrape the leg bones of Lupey and Ruthie. "It's some kinda infection," Rickets told her, "that comes back and has t'be scraped away."

"Been here near two years, yessir," Rickets bragged. "But a'm a-goin' home some time soon, ah hope, ah hope, hope, hope." She had a grin that made one come on your face whether you felt like it or not. And her hair, what there was of it, stood up straight like a haystack in a windstorm. Alice Ann wrote about Rickets in her diary.

She wrote, too, that having polio wasn't so bad, compared to bone problems like Lupey's and Ruthie's. *She* was going to get better, with the physio-therapy. It hurt a little sometimes, the leg-liftings by the hundreds and leg-stretchings the same. Being in the swim tank was best of all, because in the water her paralyzed legs could move! It was wonderful to make them go back and forth, up and down like before she had polio.

First time in the tank, Alice Ann thought she'd been miraculously healed, like Jesus did it. She was all of a sudden not dead in her legs! Not needing the physiotherapist to lift or guide them. But the minute she was lifted from the tank, she was back into the numbness. Crying wouldn't help, so she didn't even let one tear out. Cooperating with Miss Amos was the thing to do to maybe walk again.

There was a lot you could do in a wheelchair. You could write poems and stories, sing, play the piano and trombone, all sorts of things. It still was sad to think about spending the rest of your life sitting down. Rickets said to think positive. Then things would turn out better. She could take your mind off worrying when she thought up fun things to do. Wheelchair races down the middle hall between Big Girls and Little Girls' wards were great. Gurney races were even better.

One night when it was late and Nurse Trulla was downstairs in the kitchen for break, Rickets helped Alice Ann get into her wheelchair, and they ever so quietly snuck down to the nurses' desk where Rickets showed her their charts in a drawer.

"Wow! Lookee this, girl-friend! Here's yours and it says 'O.K. for surgery.' Say, maybe you're up fer operation like Jenny Lou was onct."

There it was, in big, important-looking words across from her date of entry, and weight and height. "O.K. FOR SURGERY." It was signed by Dr. Orr, the head of everything and the very first doctor to examine her.

Dr. Orr was small, like Daddy, with a kind smile and hands soft as a lady's. He told her that he had a red-haired daughter like her, and she liked him right away. The other one, Dr. Alcorn, was abrupt and scratchy-voiced with the longest nose, like an eagle's beak. He had twisted her legs roughly and used a wooden hammer to knock up and down her backbone, not saying a word. Then he cleared his throat, "humphed" and "ummmed" and wrote on a clipboard he carried.

Maybe Dr. Alcorn was the one who wrote "O.K. for Surgery" on Alice Ann's chart. She really started worrying about it, but heard Nurse Trulla coming back up the ramp from eleven o'clock break and smelling of cigarettes. Alice Ann and Rickets scooted back to bed, but it was a long time to get to sleep, what with doing what Grandpa C. calling "fretting." That was a word sounding scrabbly and worrisome ... fret ... fret ... fret."

Inside her head, Alice Ann told herself that she wasn't any stranger to surgery. Four years ago, she'd had it to make her recover from double p. If it took that long to get over poliomyelitis, she should "get on with it," like Aunt Netta always said. Remembering Aunt Netta's kitchen didn't help the fretting go away. It'd be easier to feel good about things if she was just home with Daddy and Mother and Ned and Jane. Those awful words, "O.K. for Surgery," were the last thing before sleep came and the first things that opened up her mind in the morning.

Just before daylight you heard the bedpan cart trundling down the hall from Little Girls. Somehow their sound made her wonder if this was The Day. The surgery day. She shivered a little when she thought about the bad thing they had done, peeking at their charts. On the day when Mother finally had to go back home, Alice Ann almost asked her about the maybe-surgery. Instead, she pushed it down inside where it lay like a big rock in her chest.

The day came when it was too heavy to stand anymore. Nurse Trulla was helping her into a clean nightgown after supper. As it slid over her head, Alice Ann mumbled the question through the material: "When am I going for surgery? We — I mean, *I* peeked into my chart at the nurses' station, and I saw it said 'O.K. for Surgery.' Do you know when it will happen? I'm sorry, I sure am sorry." The last words came out in a rush like a waterfall.

Nurse Trulla pulled the nightgown straight, making the strangest sound, kind of like a chicken cackling. Then, "My word, child! You saw your chart? Naughty, naughty!" shaking her finger and laughing at the same time, like it was a joke. It couldn't be that funny, unless there was a mistake like a mix-up in charts somewhere. Nurse Trulla left her there for a little while, making Alice Ann worry all the more. Soon she was back, sitting alongside the bed on a stool.

"Miss Conger ... Miss Meddling Conger, you had *no* business being at Nurses' Station unattended, plus *after* hours! However, since you've seen your chart and obviously sweated a bit ..." Here her voice got soft and a little sorry-sounding, "You need to know that there's no surgery to worry your pretty head over. O.K. for surgery simply means that should there ever be a reason someday for it, well, your physical condition is okay for it. That's all. Understand?"

It was then that Nurse Trulla pushed the stool out into the middle of Big Girls' Ward, climbed up on it and said in a very loud voice: **"Give me your attention, ladies! As of this moment, Nurses' Station is OFF LIMITS to you immediately past last bedpan shift! Do I make myself clear? I say, is that clear?"**

Down both sides of the room from all the beds and some wheelchairs, came the words tumbling over each other: "Yes, ma'am, Nurse Trulla … Yes, Nurse … Yes, Trulla … Yes." Plus some giggling. There were sighs of relief from Alice Ann and from Rickets, who'd been listening all the while.

* * * * * * * * * *

Thinking about it, Alice Ann decided that one of the bad things about being at Orthopedic was the loneliness. Oh sure, letters from home and cards from friends were swell. Mail time was something to look forward to. She tried to get over the loneliness by writing in her diary all the good things, like when they got to go down to the courtyard behind the building for their "sunning." Boys from Big Boys' Ward above them got to come, too. They could sit in wheelchairs or lie on gurneys soaking up the afternoon sun, talking and even flirting a bit. The Big Girls' Ward patients who'd been at Orthopedic a long time knew all the boys and kidded around with them, like old friends. The only trouble was there weren't many warm enough days to go outside and enjoy the fellowship.

Kids at Orthopedic needed sun every day, so on cloudy days they went up to Top Floor for being exposed to special infrared lamps. Sunglasses were necessary and flimsy cotton petticoats. Nurse Bertha called them "shifts," and you got segregated from the boys, since they were so thin, Alice Ann imagined.

The most interesting of the Big Boys was the one they all called "Doc." He swore he was only sixteen, but his head was as bald as a grandpa's. He told Alice Ann that he'd never have any hair. Doc lay on a gurney since he couldn't sit up, but he talked about astronomy and then photography when he found out about Alice Ann living and working in a studio. She determined to pray for Doc to get well enough to walk again, like she was praying to God every night about Rickets.

Mother would write and ask: "Now how's your little friend, Crickets?" never saying her name right. It was hard to tell her that Rickets was on a gurney all the time now, because she wasn't strong enough to run her wheelchair.

Before the gurney, when the two of them went tootling down the hall together, Alice Ann decided it might not be so bad to be in a wheelchair forever. You could go just about anywhere. Saturdays she and Rickets took their wheelchairs to the Clothes Closet Room where all Big Girls' clothing hung on rods. They each wheeled in under the clothes, smack-dab against the wall to sit very quiet and hidden. The reason was Texas Mary, who came to entertain the "pore little crippled childern." She would rush in Saturday mornings, with her fur coat and cowboy hat and her guitar. Alice Ann thought maybe she'd heard her over the little beige radio she had now.

Neither Rickets nor Alice Ann liked country style music, at least sung the way Texas Mary did, all loud and twangy. They'd sit there with their heads in hanging nightgowns, trying hard not to giggle, but pretty soon one would start and couldn't stop even with their hands over their ears until Texas Mary left.

Nurse Trulla even knew what Rickets and Alice Ann did to get out of hearing the singing. The first time she found them she didn't say a word, just put away the clean clothes. They thought for sure she'd drag them out and back into Big Girls' Ward to be cheered up by the country music. She cleared her throat and looked a little surprised at seeing Alice Ann, still as a mouse in between two bathrobes. But she straightened them and pulled a robe across to hide Rickets better. From that moment on, Alice Ann loved her even more than she had before.

Together, coming back from movies in the guest room, Rickets always smiled a crooked smile and chanted her little chant: "Hey, Girl-Fren', 'm goin' home soon, hope-ah-hope-ah-hope," and Alice Ann said a prayer that Rickets would soon be strong enough.

Early mornings with the hum of cars driving on busy South Street was the best time to lie in bed and sort things out to decide what kind of a day it would be. That is, if you had what Grandpa C. called your "druthers."

Most of life so far had been filled with taking orders, from Mother, Daddy, teachers, ministers, doctors and the public, whose orders helped keep the studio going. It would be a real plus with being adult: able to *give* orders. Her turn was coming.

Once she got grown up, Alice Ann would be in charge and it would be good! Right now was such a "waiting for orders" time: waiting to get well, to walk, waiting for physio-therapy session, waiting for breakfast tray, for the bedpan, the mail from home, the day's news over her little beige radio.

Another thing to be waited for and handled as best she ever could was school. Dr. Alcorn decided she was well enough to attend classes upstairs with other Big Girls and Boys. Sign-up for Latin, English and math back home helped make the decision to try to learn enough to maybe catch up with the freshman class at Loup City High.

Letters from Ellen said that Latin was hard, but there was this cute guy from Catholic who'd been an altar boy in church and had a headstart understanding and speaking Latin. Reading Ellen's letters brought on homesickness and wondering. What if she didn't get back to walking by second semester?

It was time to learn all you could, taking notes all the time, especially Latin. They added art to Alice Ann's curriculum. What an important-sounding word: curriculum. Art instructor was Mr. Sinclair who looked like Tyrone Power and spoke like Clark Gable. Nurse Trulla teased her about having a crush on Mr. S., and she guessed it was true. He knew an awful lot about artists and their paintings. He made everything interesting since he'd actually been to Paris and brought back honest-to-God art done by dead painters a long time ago.

There was a challenge, though, when Mr. Sinclair began to teach drawing. They used charcoal at first, but it was too messy and they changed to pencil. She wanted to sketch Mr. Sinclair since he was a perfect subject. One problem with it was he didn't let anyone use erasers to get rid of lines that didn't need to be there. No erasers were allowed, and finally Alice Ann got up enough nerve to ask him why.

"There's a very good reason for it, students. It's a lesson to learn. Once you make a mark, it's there to incorporate into your sketch. It's like life; once you make a mistake, it's there for good. You can't erase it. You can try to forget it, pretend it's not there, or you can learn from it and work it into your life. Now finish your sketch and remember the lesson."

Part of growing up, she decided, was disappointment with something and not showing it as much as little kids did. Mother was good at it, mostly because she always looked at the good side of things, even when they didn't turn out the way you kind of wanted them to. Mother didn't complain about not having the money for a new Easter hat or not living in a fancy house. Aunt Belle next door was different, always griping to anyone about what she didn't have. Uncle Ashley only laughed. He was more grown up than Aunt Belle who couldn't keep her disappointment to herself, like Mother did.

Mother brought the birthday cake on the Sunday before Alice Ann's real-life celebrating day. It was kind of a test in growing up and being happy with things the way they were. It would have been nice to celebrate on the *real* day, her own special day, and not four days ahead. But this was a kind of test, being able to smile and "ooh" and "ahh" over the lavender housecoat Mother had made for her, and the stationery Ned picked out and the little glass kitten from Jane Ellen.

Becoming grown up involved a bunch of tests that needed to be passed, Alice Ann knew down deep, and the birthday thing was only a little one. There would come the test of going back to school in a wheelchair maybe or on crutches. There would be the test of having people look at you and feel sorry for you the way Texas Mary did every Saturday morning.

166

The best thing to do was to be happy that Doc would bring Mother the 185 miles on Sunday; that Daddy could be busy back at the studio catching up on all the photo work; that there was enough cake for each of the girls a piece; most of all Mother saying maybe they'd all be together at home for Thanksgiving.

On her *real* birthday, Alice Ann opened six birthday cards that came in the mail, one with a dollar. She didn't mention to anyone, not even Rickets, that this was the honest-to-God day. It didn't even feel like her birthday, what with classes and physio-therapy to be busy with.

Miss Amos, in charge of physio-therapy, was always promising that no matter how hard the sessions were, healthy movement of her legs was "right around the corner." She would lift and stretch and turn and push until Alice Ann was ready to yell: "Stop! Just stop it right now!"

Alice Ann dreamed about the pushing and stretching; there was the one dream about being in a long, dark tunnel, a closed-in feeling where she'd be crawling on hands and knees. Miss Amos would be somewhere calling out for her to stand up, but she couldn't, hard as she'd try. Then she'd look down and, oh dear, there wouldn't be anything past her knees. The rest of her legs would be gone and a scream would come from inside the tunnel, maybe Miss Amos yelling at her, but then it would echo inside her own head and she'd wake up.

Dr. Alcorn was the one who always came into Big Girls unexpectedly. He would walk to each girl's bed with their charts in his hand. When he reached Alice Ann, he'd help her into the wheelchair and ask her to do only one thing: cross her legs. Before polio, crossing your legs had been so easy, putting one leg over the top of the other knee. But now it was the hardest thing in the world. She guessed maybe those leg muscles were the worst paralyzed. Dr. Alcorn would stand beside her and all he would say was: "WELL?" She knew what he wanted, so with all her might Alice Ann would try and try and try again, sometimes even grinding her teeth together. But nothing would happen, and everybody there knew it wasn't her turn to go home yet.

One day it was a real surprise to see Rickets being rolled down the hall toward the Guests' Room next to the elevator, where Alice Ann had wheeled herself to practice playing the piano. Someone had left sheet music there, and it was easy to sight-read. She was doing pretty well when she saw Rickets on the gurney with Nurse Bertha guiding while an orderly pushed. Rickets had her coat on and stocking cap and mittens. She did a little wave toward Alice Ann and said in her littlest voice, "Goin' home, girl friend, like ah said. Hot diggity."

Into the elevator she went, and Nurse Bertha stood beside it until the door shut on the orderly and Rickets. She turned to Alice Ann and said the *most AWFUL* thing! She smiled a sad kind of smile, turned away to go, but said loud enough for Alice Ann to understand. She said, "Goin' home, yeah. Goin' home to *die.*"

* * * * * * * * * *

The biggest, most important test of all came when she least expected it. Somehow, she'd been waiting so long, hoping so long that it seemed like her life would always be a bunch of "maybe tomorrows" all strung out like Christmas tree lights waiting to be turned on.

The appointment with Dr. Orr was postponed three different times; once when his vacation came up, then an emergency in his family, and then one of the doctors at Orthopedic died. There needed to be what the nurses called a "consensus," which meant that three doctors had to be in on any kind of decision.

So by the time the doctors finally showed up in Physio-Therapy, it was a tremendous surprise. Miss Amos was with Alice Ann at the bars, walking alongside and giving her encouragement to use legs that were getting stronger all the time. Now they moved when she willed them to! They were beginning to act like regular legs. Sometimes they tingled, and then she leaned against the bar and waited. Most times all that she needed to do was to guide her body along the track, barely touching the bars. Miss Amos called it "Touch 'n' go, girl, touch 'n' go." Now she could go the whole distance without falling down or leaning too much.

Miss Amos had just wheeled the wheelchair around for Alice Ann to sit in when there came Dr. Orr, the red-faced old dear, like he'd been running upstairs, all out of breath. He should probably lose some weight, she thought, but kept it to herself. The doctor Alice Ann had never seen before watched and listened to every word Dr. Orr and Dr. Alcorn said, writing things in a big blue notebook. He came over with Dr. Alcorn to the wheelchair and, sure enough, Dr. Eagle's Beak put his hands on his hips and said his favorite word: "Well?" She knew exactly what Dr. Alcorn wanted, like before. It was the big test, to see if one leg could lift and move over the other knee.

She found that it still wasn't easy, but Alice Ann

thought a little prayer and concentrated like nobody's business. She sat straight and still, taking a deep breath, with hands on the wheelchair's arms, wanting to reach down and help, but not daring. There was one long moment when it seemed like it couldn't happen, but she kept on target. Almost like magic, her right leg lifted up a little and went back down, but lifted again and over the top of her left knee and went back down without even a thump. Miss Amos clapped and Dr. Orr smiled. Dr. Alcorn did one of his "Humph's," so she did the same thing with Lefty. It was better, right over on top of her right knee, but her chest felt tight and her head began to ache.

"We saw you walking down the hall," Dr. Orr said. "With crutches, you can go back, Alice Ann, from whence you came, and I'll see you at the Hastings Clinic in January. Miss Amos, do instruct your patient in the crutch use and give her copies of follow-up exercises. I want her to roll on the floor regularly, at least twice a day … maybe resume school for half-days using her crutches at all times for one month; no stair-climbing for that period. Alice Ann, we've notified your parents to come for you and will give more instructions at that time. We just don't want to see you around the place anymore."

His eyes crinkled, and she could tell by the tone of Dr. Orr's voice that he was very pleased to be sending her home. Home! A place she hadn't seen for two months, almost! The Orthopedic was a swell place to recover in, but it wasn't the same with Rickets gone.

Wow! Alice Ann wanted to reach out and put both arms around Dr. Orr, even around Dr. Alcorn, but she was too shy. Did they know how happy they'd made her? It was for sure the happiest moment in her whole life. Later, the only way she could describe it in her diary was a big beautiful window being opened into all her tomorrows. Alice Ann knew that she now could do almost anything she'd ever dreamed of doing.

With that window opened up and promising she would walk with strong legs, maybe dance with them, especially march with them in band, why, the world was a lovely place, almost like heaven. If she shut her eyes, she could imagine God and angels smiling all around and singing: "Goin' home, Alice Ann, goin' home." And one of the angels would be Rickets, still saying, "Ah-hope, ah-hope, ah-hope."

• For Harriet Joy Potter-Conger •

How have you loved me?
Let me count the ways ...

Through summers, autumns,
springs and winters of our days ...

Through fevers and paralysis,
through lungs collapsed,

through strengthened limbs
with faith synapsed.

Through first loves, in-betweens,
with counsel to believe in dreams.

Through loss of loved ones,
and through tears;

through laughter echoing
down our sweet years.

In studio and garden,
youth and whitened hair,

In promises you made
to still be there.

You've loved with such a love
as only daughters know

from mothers who remember love
passed on to them long, long ago.

— Alice Ann